Dr. Debra Clary

Foreword by Jack Stahl,
former president and COO of The Coca-Cola Company

THE
CURIOSITY
CURVE

A Leader's Guide to
Growth and Transformation
Through Bold Questions

FAST
COMPANY
Press

This publication is designed to provide accurate and authoritative information in regard to the subject matter covered. It is sold with the understanding that the publisher and author are not engaged in rendering legal, accounting, or other professional services. Nothing herein shall create an attorney-client relationship, and nothing herein shall constitute legal advice or a solicitation to offer legal advice. If legal advice or other expert assistance is required, the services of a competent professional should be sought.

Fast Company Press
New York, New York
www.fastcompanypress.com

Copyright © 2025 Debra Clary
All rights reserved.

Thank you for purchasing an authorized edition of this book and for complying with copyright law. No part of this book may be reproduced, stored in a retrieval system, or transmitted by any means, electronic, mechanical, photocopying, recording, or otherwise, without written permission from the copyright holder.

This work is being published under the Fast Company Press imprint by an exclusive arrangement with Fast Company. Fast Company and the Fast Company logo are registered trademarks of Mansueto Ventures, LLC. The Fast Company Press logo is a wholly owned trademark of Mansueto Ventures, LLC.

Distributed by Greenleaf Book Group

For ordering information or special discounts for bulk purchases, please contact Greenleaf Book Group at PO Box 91869, Austin, TX 78709, 512.891.6100.

Design and composition by Greenleaf Book Group and Carlos Esparza
Cover design by Greenleaf Book Group and Carlos Esparza
Original icons by Aarron Mayper

Publisher's Cataloging-in-Publication data is available.
Print ISBN: 978-1-63908-138-7
eBook ISBN: 978-1-63908-139-4

To offset the number of trees consumed in the printing of our books, Greenleaf donates a portion of the proceeds from each printing to the Arbor Day Foundation. Greenleaf Book Group has replaced over 50,000 trees since 2007.

Printed in the United States of America on acid-free paper
25 26 27 28 29 30 31 32   10 9 8 7 6 5 4 3 2 1
First Edition

CONTENTS

Foreword   v
Introduction: Are You Curious?   1

PART I: CURIOUS ABOUT CURIOSITY   17

Chapter 1: The Nature of Curiosity   19
Chapter 2: The Neuroscience of Curiosity   43
Chapter 3: Curiosity Is Good Business   61

PART II: THE CURIOSITY CURVE   85

Chapter 4: The Four Factors of Curious Companies   87
Chapter 5: Exploration   121
Chapter 6: Focused Engagement   141
Chapter 7: Inspirational Creativity   161
Chapter 8: Openness to New Ideas   171

Conclusion: The Future of Curiosity   179
Resources   183
Acknowledgments   189
Notes   191
Index   197
About the Author   205

Foreword

Over the course of my career—whether leading teams at Coca-Cola or serving as CEO of Revlon—I've come to realize that the most enduring advantage in leadership isn't found in a strategy deck or a financial model. It's found in a question.

The best leaders I've worked with—those who inspired trust, sparked innovation, and built resilient cultures—shared one trait: They were relentlessly curious. They asked thoughtful questions. They listened without an agenda. And they never stopped learning, even at the top.

That's why I've long respected Deb Clary.

We first met during our time at Coca-Cola, and even then, Deb stood out—not just for her intelligence and drive, but for her ability to ask the kind of questions that moved conversations forward. She was the kind of leader who could read a room, spark ideas, and connect people in ways that made teams stronger.

That same instinct has carried through every chapter of her career—from corporate executive to TEDx speaker to performing her one-woman show, *A Curious Woman*, Off-Broadway. Across all of it, she's stayed true to her mission:

helping people and organizations unlock their potential through the power of curiosity.

The Curiosity Curve is the culmination of that work.

This book captures what many leaders feel but rarely name: that curiosity isn't a soft skill—it's a strategic imperative. Through research, real-world examples, and a practical assessment tool, Deb gives readers a clear path to strengthening their curiosity—and by extension, their leadership.

In a time when we're all encouraged to move fast and know the answers, this book invites us to pause, ask better questions, and truly listen.

Whether you're a CEO, a team leader, or simply someone seeking to grow, *The Curiosity Curve* offers the insight and tools to help you lead with more clarity, courage, and connection.

I'm honored to introduce it—and Deb—to you.

—JACK STAHL,
former president and COO of The Coca-Cola Company

Introduction

ARE YOU CURIOUS?

It was the late 1980s, and I had just been promoted to regional sales manager at Frito-Lay—a milestone I had worked tirelessly to achieve. Five years earlier, fresh out of business school, I was armed with ambition, confidence, and a vision of stepping into a leadership role right away. But reality had other plans.

My first job offer wasn't in management—it was as a Frito-Lay route driver. Instead of leading a team, I joined Teamsters Local Union No. 337, driving a truck through the streets of Detroit, delivering potato chips. It wasn't what I had envisioned, but that truck became my greatest classroom. I mastered Profit & Loss management, built relationships with store managers and back-door receivers, and learned how to sell from the ground up. That hands-on experience set me apart when I finally stepped into leadership. Now, as a regional sales manager, I was determined to prove that real leadership isn't just about strategy—it's about understanding the business from every angle.

Our global marketing team wanted to expand beyond their signature salty snacks and venture into a new category: sweet treats. Launching a new product line in a competitive market required an enormous investment—research, marketing, and promotional campaigns were set in motion, all backed by millions of dollars.

My role? Ensure the flawless rollout of this high-stakes launch. But my biggest challenge was winning over the route drivers—a critical group. These drivers, represented by the Teamsters Union, had a lot of sway over any changes to their routes. This was especially true because of a crippling strike just a few years earlier that had left deep scars. They were already stretched thin, and I had to convince them that adding a new line of cookies to their deliveries wouldn't just mean extra work; it could mean extra income in the form of commissions.

But that was easier said than done.

Determined to avoid another standoff, I decided that instead of simply telling them how things would go, I'd ask questions. *Maybe*, I thought, *if I was curious about their point of view, we could work together to find a solution.* So, I invited the most vocal and influential drivers to a focus group.

I started by laying out the opportunity: Frito-Lay's dominance in salty snacks could give us an edge in the growing sweet category. I showed off slick marketing materials highlighting the new products, and then I asked, "How do you see us making this work?"

Immediately, the objections poured in. "No room on the trucks," they said. "Too heavy. Too many stops. We'll have to service more locations—it's not worth the extra time."

I didn't argue. Instead, I got up and began writing their concerns on a flip chart. "This is good," I said. "Keep going. What else?" Once they'd aired all of their frustrations and we had a board full of reasons why it wouldn't work, I paused.

"We all want to see a little extra money in our paychecks, right? How might we tackle these challenges?"

There was a long, uncomfortable silence. But curiosity has a way of filling the space. Finally, one driver spoke up. "What if corporate designed special racks to make room for the cookies on the trucks?" he asked.

> **Curiosity has a way of filling the space.**

I wrote it down. Another chimed in with, "Maybe we can stagger the delivery times, so it doesn't all hit at once." I wrote that down too. One by one, solutions started to emerge. What began as a wall of resistance turned into a collaborative brainstorming session.

By the end of the meeting, we had a plan. And not just any

plan—it was *their* plan. It was born out of curiosity, out of asking the right questions and creating space for new ideas to surface.

The result? We achieved one of the highest route sales averages across the country. I was invited by senior executives to come to Frito-Lay headquarters to share our strategy on how we accomplished this outstanding achievement.

The workplace has evolved a lot since the 1980s, but as you probably know well, traditional approaches still hold sway, and we're often not encouraged to truly think outside the box. If you've been working for many years, you may have the power to implement change. Or maybe you've met so much resistance from peers and higher-ups who are stubbornly set in their ways that pushing for change seems like more than you can take on. And if you're earlier in your career, you might not feel empowered to push much at all.

Say you've just taken on your first team lead role, managing a small but growing group. You've proven yourself by meeting deadlines, increasing efficiency, and exceeding quarterly goals. Now, you've been tasked with leading a new project: launching a new product aimed at a demographic you're not entirely familiar with. You're confident in your skills, but this market is different, and you suspect that tried-and-true methods might not work. You're feeling the pressure to deliver results—fast.

As you sit in your office reviewing the latest data, your instinct is to dive in head-first and stick to the proven strategies that have worked in the past, which got you in the position you are now. But again, the situation feels different.

What if, instead of assuming you have all the answers, you approached this from a place of curiosity?

You decide to reach out to your team. At your next meeting, instead of outlining a rigid plan, you open with questions: "Given constraints, how could we make this work? What are we *not* asking? What if we ask questions here today, with no attachment to the answers?"

At first, there's hesitation. Some team members give cautious, surface-level responses, while others stay silent. After all, this isn't how you've started a project before. But you let the awkwardness linger for a minute, letting the possibility for curiosity bloom.

"Let's dig deeper," you suggest. "What do we think this customer wants? What's important to them? Their values? Their preferences? What's missing from our current strategy, and what adjustment would benefit us and them?"

Now, the energy in the room begins to shift. Your team starts throwing out ideas—some of which you've never considered before.

"Well, there's this new digital platform trending with that group right now," one team member offers.

"And you know," someone else says, getting a bit bolder, "they might think our brand is just a little bit dated."

"Okay, so how can we refresh it?" you ask. Now they're off: You keep asking questions, guiding the discussion but listening and encouraging even the most outlandish ideas, and writing everything down on a flip chart (some old methods do still work, after all).

By the end of the meeting, you don't just have a strategy; you have an innovative, team-driven approach. You've uncovered insights that weren't visible in the data. And best of all, your team feels more engaged, and they're clearly excited about the direction you're heading.

> Most of us have become so focused on having the answers that we have forgotten how to ask questions.

Most of us have become so focused on *having the answers* that we have forgotten how to ask questions—how to genuinely understand each other. Curious people find a way to shift urgency to exploration. By stepping back, we can unlock potential that's hiding in plain sight.

That's the transformative power of curiosity. It's not just about solving problems—it's about empowering others to think differently, collaborate, and discover solutions together.

And we *need* curiosity, now more than ever. As you'll learn in the pages to come, stifling curiosity has wide implications for how we relate to one another and our communities. This is a book about how to find your curiosity again—in the workplace and in your life in general.

※

We're all born curious—everything around us is new, and we instinctively seek to understand it. But along the way, that curiosity fades. We're not just discouraged from asking questions—we're taught to be incurious. It starts early, with messages like *children should be seen and not heard*, and continues into adulthood, where work demands, pressure, and rigid expectations leave little room for exploration. Over time, curiosity isn't just forgotten—it's unlearned.

One of the people who reminded me of the profound importance of curiosity was my daughter, Madeline. When she was a freshman in high school, just as the winter sports season began, she decided to try out for the varsity girls' basketball team. It was an audacious goal that, at first glance, seemed out of reach. By her own admission, Madeline couldn't dribble, shoot, or run particularly fast. And from what I had seen, her assessment was accurate. After all, dribbling, shooting, and speed are pretty crucial skills for any basketball player. Yet, as her mother, my instinct was to help her pursue her dream. She wanted to make that team, and my role was to support her in every way I could. I had encouraged both my daughters to go for their dreams. Be bold; proceed until apprehended, and let your actions resonate with unwavering determination, forging a path that inspires others to follow.

I started brainstorming conventional ways to improve her skills: attending a basketball camp, hiring a private coach, or practicing together in our driveway. But Madeline quickly dismissed my suggestions with an annoyed, "That won't work!"

Surprised, I asked, "Why not?"

She looked at me with a seriousness that stopped me in my tracks. "Tryouts are Monday," she said. We had only two days.

Confused, I pressed further, "Why is this so important to you? Why now, in your freshman year?"

After a long pause, tears welled in her eyes as she finally said, "This is my last chance to play on the same team as my sister. Megan is a senior."

In that moment, I understood. Her drive wasn't fueled by a desire for a varsity letter; it was about sharing one final season with her sister before Megan went off to college. Hearing her heartfelt "why" ignited a deep passion within me. I knew her why, and I was determined to help her make that team. Drawing on my two decades of experience in marketing, I rolled up my sleeves and got to work. I taped a large piece of flip chart paper to the wall, grabbed a black marker, and said, "Madeline, let's make a plan."

I began by asking, "You play varsity volleyball. What skills do you use there that could transfer to varsity basketball?"

She thought for a moment and then said, "Well, I'm an outside hitter, so I guess I can jump."

I nodded. "Exactly! And basketball players need to jump." I wrote *jump* on the flip chart. "When you jump to the top of the net, what are you doing?" I asked.

"Spiking the ball," she replied.

"Right, and that's called hand-eye coordination—another important skill for basketball." I added *hand-eye coordination* to the list. "And when you're in the back row on defense, what are you doing?" I asked.

"Digging out balls," she said.

"Yes! That's hustle, and basketball players need hustle." I wrote *hustle* on the chart.

The list read: *jump, hand-eye coordination,* and *hustle.* I turned to her and asked one more question: "Madeline, I'm curious—what else do you have that could contribute to the varsity basketball team?"

She paused for a moment, then smiled and said, "I think that's it. It's a solid list."

I looked at her and asked, "Do you think being tall would be helpful?"

Her eyes widened with realization. "Oh yeah, I'm tall!" she exclaimed. I added it to the list.

Madeline had completely overlooked one of her greatest strengths. Sometimes, our most valuable assets are the ones we take for granted—and without someone to remind us, they can go unnoticed.

We examined her strengths with fresh eyes and built her confidence, but that was only the beginning. We needed a strategy that would showcase her strengths and minimize her weaknesses. I taped a second sheet of paper labeled *TRYOUTS* to the wall. "On Monday," I said, "you're going to hustle down the court, plant yourself under the basket, jump, rebound, and pass the ball. Jump, rebound, pass the ball. Dribbling and shooting—that's not you." She looked at me and smiled, a newfound confidence lighting up her face.

Empowered by this plan, Madeline went into tryouts with conviction. That confidence resonated with the coach. Not only did she make the varsity team, but she also went on to become the leading rebounder in the school's history—boys and girls alike.

This is the power of curiosity. It uncovers hidden potential and reframes challenges as opportunities. Despite the flood of messages we receive through advertising and social media about the power we hold within, many of us still hesitate to take risks or step into the unknown. We often curb our curiosity, remembering the adage: "Curiosity killed the cat." But the full proverb is "Curiosity killed the cat, but satisfaction brought it back."

Madeline's story is a powerful reminder that even the smallest sparks of belief, fueled by curiosity and encouragement, can ignite a journey that changes everything. Yes, curiosity can be scary, but the satisfaction it brings is all the sweeter, leading us to discoveries and growth we never knew we needed.

※

In today's fast-paced business world, curiosity is increasingly recognized for its transformative power and inherent value. Leadership has evolved beyond simply making decisions and issuing directives; it now demands fostering a culture where questioning, innovation, and collaboration are not just encouraged but embedded into the fabric of the organization. This is the approach I championed at Frito-Lay and one that is reflected in the story of the new manager guiding her team toward innovation. Without the capacity for employees to embrace and act on their curiosity, an organization risks losing its competitive edge.

Yet, while the importance of curiosity is acknowledged, sustaining it within a company culture presents significant challenges. I recently spoke with the new CEO of a prominent healthcare technology company. Having ascended through the ranks alongside the company's founder, she was handpicked as his successor when he reached his late seventies.

However, she quickly discovered that the organization's deeply ingrained culture didn't align with her vision. With most of the 17,000 employees having spent decades adhering to the founder's strict, top-down decision-making style, they were unaccustomed to offering their own insights or opinions. When she posed questions like "What do you think?" during meetings, the response was often an uneasy silence.

Realizing that true change would require more than just words, she embraced the need to model curiosity consistently. This meant trusting in her team's capabilities, implementing their suggestions where possible, and, when it wasn't feasible, working collaboratively to explain why. It also involved empowering employees to make decisions and fostering an environment where outcomes—successful or otherwise—were learning experiences, not grounds for blame. Through these actions, she is gradually nurturing a shift toward a more participatory and innovative culture.

Change on this scale is never instantaneous, but early signs are already evident. Among those 17,000 employees, a few brave individuals are beginning to respond, drawn by the promise of a more open and inquisitive work environment. They are starting to voice their ideas and test the waters, though not without some trepidation. The lingering question on their minds is: "What will happen if I push too far? Could my job be at risk?"

This tension is not unique to her company; I see it frequently in the broader business landscape. Too often, employees stifle their curiosity, feeling constrained by a lack of time and support, or by a culture that values compliance over innovation. Yet the desire for curiosity remains powerful and undeniable. The Great Resignation of 2022–2023, coupled with the "quiet quitting" movement (where employees do the bare minimum), highlighted that many, especially those under 40, refuse to commit to workplaces where curiosity is stifled. They seek environments that encourage their creative input and exploration, signaling that the future of work will favor organizations that make room for curiosity, engagement, and active participation.

> Gallup's research highlights a concerning trend: employee disengagement is taking an increasingly severe toll on the US economy. What was once a $1 trillion drain now costs the economy an estimated $8.9 trillion annually.[1] This escalation underscores the urgent need for organizations to foster environments that engage and inspire their workforce, turning potential loss into growth and productivity.

At the heart of this movement are millennials, the dynamic force of the workforce, who comprise 36% of the US employee base.[2] Many feel disconnected, undervalued, and disengaged. When asked why, their top response is that nobody seems genuinely interested in what sparks their curiosity.[3] Their ideas, perspectives, and potential solutions are often met with silence. It supports the adage that "those closest to the solution are often least consulted."

Imagine what could happen if we intentionally flipped the script—replacing complacency with curiosity at every level of an organization. To explore this potential, I commissioned Lab 201 to conduct original research examining how curiosity intersects with leadership and performance. Our study focused on four key dimensions that would eventually form the foundation of what we call the Curiosity Curve®: exploration, focused engagement, inspirational creativity, and openness to new ideas.

In collaboration with Lab 201's founder and director, Cory Kim—a former neuroscience researcher at the University of Tokyo—we developed the Cultural Curiosity Scale (CCS), a tool designed to measure how well employees feel their curiosity is encouraged and supported at work. The results were eye-opening; revealing hidden dynamics and patterns that traditional engagement surveys often miss.

The findings, illustrated in part in Figure 1.1, demonstrate the power of curiosity. Each mark in the scatter plot represents an individual participant in our comprehensive survey. The upward trend of the curve highlights that employees working in environments where curiosity is supported report higher job satisfaction. This job satisfaction correlates with improved financial performance and successful innovation.

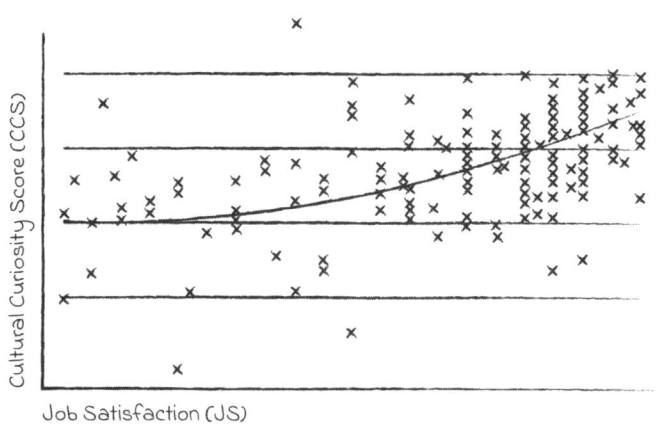

Figure 1.1: The Curiosity Curve
Source: Lab 201, Curiosity Curve survey, 2023

From Socrates to Plato, philosophers have long wrestled with the question: What makes someone successful? Our findings revealed a strong connection between a culture that nurtures curiosity and key performance indicators such as employee engagement, job satisfaction, and retention. This aligns with research from Sophie von Stumm, director of the Hungry Mind Lab at the University of York, whose work suggests that curiosity plays a crucial role in individual success. Her meta-analysis of 200 studies indicates that curiosity—when combined with conscientiousness—can be just as influential as intelligence in driving achievement.[4]

Throughout history, success has often been attributed to intelligence or discipline alone. But research now shows that a mindset driven by learning, persistence, and exploration is just as critical. By fostering curiosity, both individuals and organizations can unlock higher levels of performance and long-term success.

Although correlation does not imply causation, the data reinforces the connection between curiosity and positive outcomes. Observations in real-world scenarios support this as well. Throughout this book, we revisit the Curiosity Curve as we explore how leaders can cultivate a workplace that thrives on curiosity, one where every voice matters, every idea is considered, and fresh perspectives are welcomed.

However, curiosity is not without its challenges. Trust is a vital component. Taking a risk—whether reaching out to touch a stove or extending a hand to a colleague—carries uncertainty. Leaders like the CEO of the healthcare technology company I mentioned must be ready for initial resistance. Passion must be balanced with patience.

Companies, too, must learn to harness their curiosity. When leaders adopt an inquisitive mindset, their organizations transform into places that are vibrant, innovative, and fulfilling to work in. Legendary examples include Apple under Steve Jobs, Patagonia under Yvon Chouinard, and Berkshire Hathaway under Warren Buffett. These companies are renowned for their leaders' curiosity and their willingness to experiment and ask "What if?"

Many companies, however, fall short. They fail to encourage the kind of curiosity that could propel them forward, leaving them vulnerable to disruption. Take Kodak, which famously overlooked digital camera technology in the 1990s, or Blockbuster, which dismissed the potential of streaming services. Within these companies, there were undoubtedly employees who were eager to explore these new ideas, but their voices were not heard.

Curiosity isn't just essential in the business sphere; it's also the bedrock of a democratic society. Democracies thrive when individuals have the freedom to make choices and actively participate in shaping their world. Curiosity guides us in this pursuit, helping us make informed decisions and seek out the path to happiness.

But without cultivating an optimal curiosity setpoint, individuals can be easily swayed, especially in an age dominated by artificial intelligence and misinformation. Leaders must engage with people and strive to understand their perspectives to foster meaningful, trustworthy interactions.

If you are in a leadership role, it's imperative to recognize this need. The drive for curiosity is not going anywhere. It's your responsibility to build a culture that encourages curiosity and supports employees in exploring their strengths. Doing so will lead to a more engaged, productive, and resilient organization.

Even if you aren't currently a leader, your curiosity will play a vital role in propelling you to leadership in the future. The next time you face a challenge that seems insurmountable, take inspiration from my daughter Madeline or the CEO who bravely fostered curiosity. Find your unique approach, amplify your strengths, engage your team, and listen closely to their input. Most importantly, let your curiosity guide you.

That's why I wrote this book: to help people dismantle the barriers that prevent them from embracing curiosity. I aim to show leaders across sectors—business, nonprofits, and government—how to harness the power of curiosity for sustainable success.

Drawing from my three decades of leadership experience as a "curiosity whisperer" in Fortune 100 companies, my doctorate in leadership development and organizational design, and even my side career as an Off-Broadway solo performer of *A Curious Woman*, this book blends scientific insights with personal stories and interviews. The chapters in Part I introduce the nature of curiosity, the neuroscience behind it, and why it is vital for business success. You also learn to develop and nurture your curiosity into an effective habit. Part II explores the four growth factors of curiosity—exploration, focused engagement, inspirational creativity, and openness to new ideas—with practical tips, self-assessments, and reflections to implement these in your workplace.

If curiosity is indeed contagious, then I hope this book spreads it like wildfire. And if you catch it, expect to gain a deeper capacity for effective action, a renewed sense of humor, and a profound sense of wonder as we explore curiosity together.

Part I

CURIOUS ABOUT CURIOSITY

Curiosity is one of the most powerful yet underestimated forces in the world. It's the spark that has driven every major breakthrough, the instinct that compels us to seek out new experiences, and the unseen force shaping how we navigate challenges. But while we celebrate curiosity in children, we often suppress it in adulthood—especially in professional settings, where efficiency, predictability, and expertise are prized over exploration, questioning, and discovery.

Yet, curiosity is not just an intellectual luxury; it's a fundamental driver of growth, problem-solving, and innovation. It's what separates stagnant organizations from thriving ones and disengaged individuals from those who are constantly evolving. Curiosity allows us to look beyond the obvious, to spot patterns others miss, and to uncover the "dogs that don't bark"—those silent but significant details that can change everything.

The good news? Curiosity isn't an innate gift reserved for a select few. It's a skill, a habit, and a mindset that anyone can develop. And just like a muscle, the more we exercise it, the stronger it becomes. Whether in leadership, collaboration, or personal development, curiosity has the power to transform how we engage with the world.

In the chapters ahead, we break curiosity down into four essential dimensions, each critical to its full expression. We begin with **exploration**, the initial spark that propels us toward new challenges and opportunities. Next, we examine **focused engagement**, the discipline to channel curiosity into meaningful, goal-oriented action. Then, we explore **inspirational creativity**, the ability to connect ideas and transform insights into innovation. Finally, we uncover the power of **openness to new ideas**, the willingness to challenge assumptions and embrace fresh perspectives.

As you move through this section, you'll discover actionable strategies, real-world examples, and thought-provoking insights to help you strengthen these dimensions in your life. Whether you're an individual contributor seeking growth or a leader striving to create a culture of curiosity, the Curiosity Curve provides a framework to harness curiosity as a tool for success.

Curiosity doesn't just shape history's greatest minds—it can shape yours too. Let's dive in.

1
THE NATURE OF CURIOSITY

One of the most famous Sherlock Holmes stories, "The Adventure of Silver Blaze," hinges on an overlooked detail that ultimately breaks the case wide open. The story begins with the sudden disappearance of Silver Blaze, a prized racehorse, from a Dartmoor stable on the eve of an important race. The horse's trainer is found dead, apparently murdered by a blow to the head.

Initially, the evidence seems to implicate an outsider—a bookmaker named Fitzroy Simpson. But Holmes is intrigued by an unusual clue: the "curious incident of the dog in the night-time." When the police detective points out that the dog did nothing during the night, Holmes responds, "That was the curious incident."[1]

The significance? If Simpson, a stranger, had approached the stable that night, the dog would have barked. The silence suggested that the culprit was someone familiar to the dog.

This pivotal observation reveals the hidden truth, showing that what *didn't* happen was just as important as what did. It leads to an essential question: In our own lives, how often do we overlook the "dogs that don't bark"—the subtle inconsistencies or omissions that, if scrutinized, could reveal deeper insights?

Curiosity is more than just asking obvious questions; it means probing deeper and seeking out what isn't immediately visible. Yet surprisingly, we often lose this instinct in both our personal and professional lives. The result? We become less engaged and more prone to boredom and frustration, and we stifle our growth. This isn't entirely our fault. Most of us are subtly conditioned to set aside our curiosity early in life and find it challenging to reconnect with it or even understand what curiosity looks like in today's fast-paced, demanding world.

In this chapter, we rediscover what curiosity truly means and learn how to invite it back into our lives. We explore why nurturing curiosity is vital for our personal fulfillment and professional success and how it can help us notice those silent dogs that might just hold the answers we've been searching for.

TRAIT OR SKILL?

What is this quality that Sherlock Holmes epitomizes? Is it a rare gift bestowed upon a lucky few, or is it something we can consciously develop—a skill that improves with practice? Too often, we're led to believe that curiosity is an innate talent, reserved for scientists, artists, or entrepreneurs. The rest of us might see ourselves as less curious, and by extension, less creative or innovative. But this perception overlooks a critical point: Curiosity is deeply intertwined with creativity. When curiosity is stifled, so is the creative process, leading to stagnation and a lack of meaningful progress. This affects not just individuals but entire teams and organizations, where innovation and problem-solving are essential for success.

Think of it this way: When you're presented with a puzzle or a mystery, do you always react the same way? Or are there some challenges that intrigue you more than others? Consider a simple riddle, like "What has keys but can't open locks?" (a piano, of course). Do you instinctively start guessing and analyzing? That's curiosity in action. It's that innate urge to ask questions, explore different angles, and dive deeper to find solutions.

Curiosity isn't a static trait; it's a behavior, an active choice we make and cultivate over time. Being human means forming assumptions and using curiosity to challenge and validate them. It's not just a state we enter by chance but a habit that grows stronger with use, like a muscle that gains strength with exercise. This practice involves attitudes, skills, and approaches that help us engage with the world in a more meaningful way. Although our upbringing, education, and professional experiences can shape how we express our curiosity, the decision to be curious remains ours to make.

> Curiosity isn't a static trait; it's a behavior, an active choice we make and cultivate over time.

Some people, like Holmes, continually exercise their curiosity. They practice it, refine it, and become adept at wielding it as a powerful tool. This process turns curiosity from a sporadic impulse into a refined skill, one that becomes second nature over time. The more we choose to be curious, the more proficient we become, eventually reaching a level where curiosity drives our greatest breakthroughs.

Throughout history, visionaries like Albert Einstein, Marie Curie, and Steve Jobs exemplified this process. They didn't treat curiosity as a mere whim but as an essential tool for exploration and problem-solving. Einstein once wrote to his biographer, "I have no special talents. I am only passionately curious."[2] For these pioneers, curiosity was a starting point that led to innovations that transformed their fields—Einstein's theory of relativity, Curie's groundbreaking work in radioactivity, and Jobs's relentless pursuit of technological perfection with Apple products.

Detectives in the real world echo this sentiment. Ivar Fahsing, a senior police detective in Oslo, Norway, and an instructor at the Norwegian Police University College, explains that exceptional investigative skills stem from metacognition—thinking about one's own thinking. He notes that the most skilled detectives don't jump to conclusions or immediately voice their opinions. Instead, they observe, ask questions, and persistently dig deeper, embodying curiosity in its most disciplined form.[3]

The Curiosity Curve study conducted for this book supports these findings, revealing that individuals working for organizations that foster curiosity score higher in personal curiosity and job satisfaction. Conversely, environments that suppress curiosity tend to diminish it, stifling not only creative potential but also overall job fulfillment and innovation. This isn't just a hypothetical scenario; it reflects real-world contrasts between workplaces that promote inquiry and those that do not.

By reframing curiosity as a skill, we can recognize its potential to drive progress and foster meaningful change. When we acknowledge that curiosity compels us to take risks—switch roles, change companies, move to new places, seek out new challenges, or even embark on new personal journeys—we start to see it as an essential part of our growth.

This ties into the concept of a "growth mindset," as described by Carol Dweck. Curiosity propels us forward, even when we're unsure of the outcome or the difficulty ahead. We persist because our desire to know what lies beyond is stronger than our fear of the unknown.[4]

Consider how this plays out in our professional lives. Curiosity drives innovative thinking and strategic problem-solving. It encourages us to ask, "What if?" and "Why not?"—questions that lead to true breakthroughs. When Einstein wondered about the relationship between space and time, it led to the theory of relativity. When Curie asked how certain elements emitted radiation, she discovered polonium and radium. When Jobs pondered how to make technology more intuitive and user-friendly, the iPhone was born.

Our surroundings influence whether we choose to cultivate our curiosity. Picture working in a rigid environment where questions are met with disapproval or where taking risks is discouraged. In contrast, imagine a workplace that celebrates ideas, supports creative exploration, and values every contribution. The difference is palpable. In the first, you might feel constrained, your curiosity stifled. In the latter, you thrive, feeling empowered to question, explore, and innovate.

The next time you find yourself in an environment that seems to stifle your curiosity, remember that feeling stuck is not a reflection of who you are. It's an indicator that you may need a change—whether that means altering your approach or seeking a new setting that fosters your curiosity.

And if you're in a position to shape the culture of your workplace or community, consider how you can create an environment that values and nurtures curiosity. This isn't just an idealistic pursuit; it's a path to transformative change. In the chapters that follow, we explore how leaders can harness the power of curiosity to inspire innovation and growth. But first, let's look at how to recognize curiosity in action and begin nurturing it in ourselves and others.

CURIOSITY SIGNALS

As we see in the next chapter, levels of curiosity can be measured: It's possible to discern an individual's level of curious behavior, as well as an organization's context for curiosity. But you don't need statistics or surveys to tell you when curiosity is in play. Here are seven tell-tale signs of curiosity that you can spot in yourself and others.

The Words People Use

I once worked with an executive coach offered by my company as part of leadership development. To better learn about myself, the coach assigned me to interview my family members about me. They were the people who knew me best. One question was: "What's my favorite word?"

Both my daughters, independently, told me I use the word "interesting." I hadn't even realized I was doing it. It was my way of saying, "I want to scratch at this a little bit more," expressing my curiosity without assigning judgment or bias. Others might use "intriguing," "curious," or "that's wild!" to mean something similar. They might even say, "I don't get it." These expressions signal that they're not just passively absorbing information but actively engaging with it, turning it over in their minds, and seeking to understand it more deeply.

Ted Lasso's quote about curiosity is "Be curious, not judgmental."[5] This simple yet profound line captures the essence of approaching others and situations with an open mind and a desire to understand rather than make assumptions.

The Questions People Ask

Curious people are masters of the art of asking questions. They ask the kinds of questions that can clear up an issue or help get to the heart of the matter. They're not interested in showing off how smart they are or catching someone in a "gotcha" moment. Instead, their questions are grounded in a genuine desire to learn, a recognition that others may see things differently, and a basic level of compassion and openness.

Here are some examples of questions with genuine curiosity behind them:

"Why does that happen?"
"What's an example?"
"What would you do differently?"
"What causes you and I to look at things differently?"

The Empathy People Feel

Empathy is the level of emotion we experience on behalf of people other than ourselves. At first glance, curiosity and empathy might seem like odd bedfellows. After all, curiosity is often associated with a certain level of detachment, of standing back and observing rather than engaging. But in reality, the two are closely intertwined. You can't truly have empathy without a certain level of curiosity.

Jamil Zaki, a professor at Stanford University who studies empathy, says there are three types of empathy, each activating different parts of the brain. Mentalizing is thinking about other people and what they're likely to do next. Experience sharing is taking into yourself some of the emotions you sense in others. Empathic concern is the commitment you make in terms of compromises or sacrifices for another person. All three require a baseline level of curiosity, because you can't invest that much in another person unless you're intrigued by them—at least enough to feel interested.[6]

The Irritation People Tolerate
Curious people can sometimes be annoying to those around them. They ask a lot of questions, they challenge assumptions, and they don't always accept things at face value. This can be frustrating for those who just want to get on with things, or who don't see the point in all this probing and prodding.

I've been there. My daughters would lay down the ground rules before I met any of their school friends. They'd say, "You get five questions. Make them good ones."

Curious cultures accept and value the explorative tendencies of their employees. They remember that irritation is often a sign that curious people are on to something. They're not just being difficult for the sake of getting noticed. They're trying to uncover some insight that others might have overlooked. And while it may be uncomfortable in the moment, that kind of curiosity can ultimately lead to breakthrough insights and innovations.

The Disruption People Cause
Curiosity throws the world apart—sometimes a little, sometimes a lot. I learned this early on, in kindergarten, in a suburb north of Detroit, Michigan. One morning, while standing in line, waiting for the bell to ring, an ice ball hit me in the eye.

For those not familiar with Northern winters, an ice ball is different from a snowball; the two should never be confused. An ice ball is a compact sphere made entirely of ice, typically denser and harder than a snowball. Unlike snowballs, which are made of loosely packed snow, ice balls are formed from solid ice or compacted and refrozen snow, making them firm and sometimes transparent.

"Aw, quit your crying, doncha know," Miss Erikson said in her Fargo accent as I ran to the front of the line. "Get back in line—you know the rules," she added.

As the day went on, my eye swelled shut. My mother, head of the school PTA, always picked me up from school. That day, instead of bundling me into the car, she looked at me with concern and said in her sweet Tennessee accent, "Child, what happened to your eye?" I explained that I had been hit by an ice ball. "Did you tell an adult, like I taught you?" she asked. I nodded and pointed to Miss Erikson, who stood nearby.

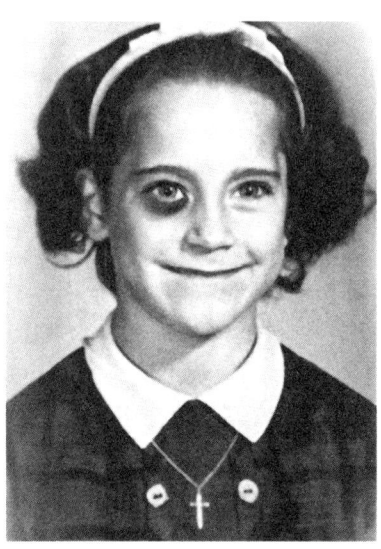

"Is this true?" my mother asked Miss Erikson, who nodded sheepishly.

Without hesitation, Mama took my hand and marched me to the school office, with Miss Erikson in tow. The principal's door was shut, but she opened it without knocking. "Principal Shepard! Excuse me for barging in, but I think you'll want to hear this. Little Debbie here was standing in line this morning when she was hit in the eye with an ice ball. She told Miss Erikson, who sent her back in line because she knew the rules." A long pause followed.

The principal, an older woman, responded with words that many officials have said to those questioning injustices: "Well, in my twenty years as principal of Lincoln Elementary School, I've never had a parent barge into my office and tell such a tale about one of our beloved teachers. You should be totally and utterly ashamed of yourself, Miss Erikson."

My young brain registered three lessons that day: first, bad things can happen when you stand in line; second, closed doors are meant to be opened; and third, my mother was a force to be reckoned with. I wanted to be just like her.

Over time, I discovered a few more truths. Power and curiosity are linked. The principal listened to my mother because she had leverage. At that moment, the meaning sank in. Disruption wasn't always bad. Yes, it made people uncomfortable, but it also called attention to what needed fixing. From that day forward, I found that being disruptive felt right, as if my purpose was to identify what was broken and push to make it better.

In the end, my curiosity became my salvation.

I discovered that I liked the feeling of being a disruptive influence or, better said, an innovator. Perhaps my purpose in the world was to find things that are broken and make them better. In any case, my curiosity was a salvation.

The Jokes People Tell

Curiosity and humor often go hand in hand. Frank Capra's classic screwball comedies, such as *Arsenic and Old Lace* and *It Happened One Night*, often start with a protagonist exercising curiosity and uncovering trouble. The same is true of classic television episodes. Elaine on *Seinfeld* is so curious about what a cartoon means that she goes to *The New Yorker* to find out.[7] In a famous John Mulaney skit on *Saturday Night Live*, Pete Davidson is warned not to order lobster in a New York diner. But he is curious enough to try.[8]

It's not just professional comedians who use humor as a signal of curiosity. We all do it to some extent. When we make a joke about something that seems strange or confusing to us, we're really just expressing our curiosity in a different way. We're saying, "I don't quite understand this, but I'm willing to engage with it and see where it takes me."

The Way People Reflect

Curious people are often highly interested in their own thinking—or, as Detective Ivar Fahsing puts it, they are "metacognitive."[9] They're not just interested in the world around them, but also in their own thoughts and beliefs. They're willing to question their own assumptions, to consider alternative perspectives, and to change their minds when presented with new evidence.

This kind of internal curiosity can be harder to spot than some of the other signs we've discussed. It's not always expressed outwardly, in the form of questions or jokes or emphatic statements. But it's no less important. In fact, it's arguably the most crucial aspect of curiosity—the willingness to turn that curious lens inward and examine our own biases, blind spots, and areas for growth.

All of these signs can indicate that curiosity is present. None of them is the full story. The next time you're in a meeting, a classroom, or even just a casual conversation, look for those signs. Listen for the language of curiosity—the probing questions, the willingness to challenge assumptions, and the reflection on one's own beliefs. And when you spot them, take a moment to appreciate the power and potential of curiosity in action.

THE CURIOSITY GAP

With all these great traits and signals, and in a world with more challenges and information than ever before, you would think that our collective curiosity is thriving. However, signs of its decline are everywhere. In most of the world, and certainly in business, there is a growing gap between the curiosity we need and the curiosity we have.

For instance, consider workplaces where employees stick to familiar processes because questioning them could be seen as disruptive or inefficient. In many educational settings, students are rewarded for following the curriculum rather than challenging it. Even in social media spaces, echo chambers often reward conformity over curiosity. The impact is profound: fewer innovative ideas, more rigid thinking, and missed opportunities for meaningful change.

The roots of this curiosity gap can probably be traced back to childhood. Infants start out innately curious. Everything is new and fascinating, and our young minds are eager to learn—not just from our parents, but from anyone nearby, such as older siblings. Cognitive scientists Alison Gopnik, Andrew Meltzoff, and Patricia Kuhl, studying young children, found that by the time they're around a year old, they become interested in everything around them, especially cues like parents pointing at things. A point is like an invitation to explore. "Evolution seems automatically to grant most children a fundamental capacity for intimacy, a profound psychological curiosity, and plenty of kinfolk to be intimate with and curious about," they write.[10]

That innate intellectual curiosity seems to erode as we get older. By the time we're adults, we may tamp it down, if only because the world around us doesn't seem to appreciate it. The problem sometimes starts with our parents. Some parents will do almost anything to avoid a curious toddler. I remember starting school when I was four years old. I was placed in kindergarten a year earlier than other children. I assumed it was because I was socially mature, emotionally stable, and intellectually advanced. Obviously. Knowing this about myself gave me such confidence—even if I didn't quite know what it meant!

Many years later, my mother confessed that she had negotiated my early acceptance with the school principal, in exchange, my mother agreed to be the president of the PTA for the next six years.

"Why," I asked, "would you do that?"

My mother replied, "Child, I just didn't think I could take another year of you constantly asking questions. You were exhausting. Every few minutes, it was something else. 'Why is the sky blue? Do fish sleep? Are all cats girls?'"

I guess I can't blame her, but parents who nurture curiosity in their children are doing a lot for posterity. In one longitudinal study that spanned 10 years, researchers found that children whose mothers encouraged them to be curious were more intellectually advanced, emotionally stable, and socially connected than their peers.[11] Curiosity is good for child development.

You can see this tension in many children's books: Babar's daughter Isabel, Eloise at the Plaza Hotel, even the Teenage

The Nature of Curiosity

Mutant Ninja Turtles and the Powerpuff Girls. Curious George epitomizes curiosity: a character who lives to push boundaries and get into mischief. It's as if parents (who buy these books, after all) are trying to strike a balance between curbing their children's relentless questioning and letting them explore.

So how do we become incurious?

We go to school. Most schools are training grounds for incuriosity. We are taught to sit still, raise our hands, and speak only when called upon. Without structure, mayhem ensues, but overemphasis on rules stifles our natural inquisitiveness. We learn to conform, to follow the curriculum, and to prioritize grades over genuine learning. Slowly but surely, our once-vibrant curiosity begins to fade.

At my elementary school, girls had to wear dresses, even during frigid Michigan winters. One day, I asked Miss Losh, my third-grade teacher, if we could wear pants. I had a hypothesis: If we were warmer, we could focus better and learn more. She pointed to the handbook and said, "Dresses only."

Undeterred, I circulated a petition and got the signatures of other girls (printed, since we hadn't learned cursive yet). I was curious to see how the school would respond. The answer, of course, was no.

Sulking at the dinner table that evening, my mother asked, "Why you so sour today, child?" I shared the disappointing news and my frustration with the "rules." She said, "Well, if they won't change the rules, find a way around them. Find a loophole. Read the handbook."

The next day, I came to school wearing pants under my dress. I was promptly sent to Principal Shepard's office. "You know the rules," she said. "Girls can't wear pants. It's clearly stated in the Lincoln Elementary Handbook."

I replied, "In due respect, it says girls have to wear dresses. And I'm wearing a dress."

My curiosity won that day. Soon, dresses over pants became a real fashion trend.

But not everyone has such triumphs. By the time we reach high school and college, the forces against curiosity become stronger. As adults entering the workforce, we are rewarded for expertise and efficiency, not for asking questions. We start to believe that curiosity is risky, a sign of carelessness or ignorance. We fear saying the wrong thing or appearing uninformed.

In some professions, experts aren't supposed to ask questions unless they already know the answers. In certain organizations, groupthink is the norm, and asking too many questions can lead to social or professional consequences.

Confirmation bias plays a role too. We tend to notice ideas that align with our existing beliefs and shy away from exploring unfamiliar territory. We might criticize others for their lack of curiosity but fail to see it in ourselves.

Our curiosity atrophies, and it's a shame. Curiosity is a predictor of success and, in the digital age, may be critical for survival. When we lose it, we lose the chance to reach our full potential and help others reach theirs.

The Johari Window model was created by Joseph Luft and Harrington Ingham in 1955.[12] It was developed as a tool to improve self-awareness, interpersonal relationships, and group dynamics. Curiosity plays a pivotal role in exploring and expanding the quadrants of the Johari Window. By fostering a mindset of curiosity, we invite opportunities to deepen our understanding of both ourselves and others. For instance, the "Blind Spot" quadrant—representing what is known to others but unknown to oneself—can be illuminated through curious engagement and open feedback. Asking questions like "How do you perceive my approach in this project?" or "What would you suggest I improve upon?" creates space for insights that are otherwise hidden.

THE JOHARI WINDOW

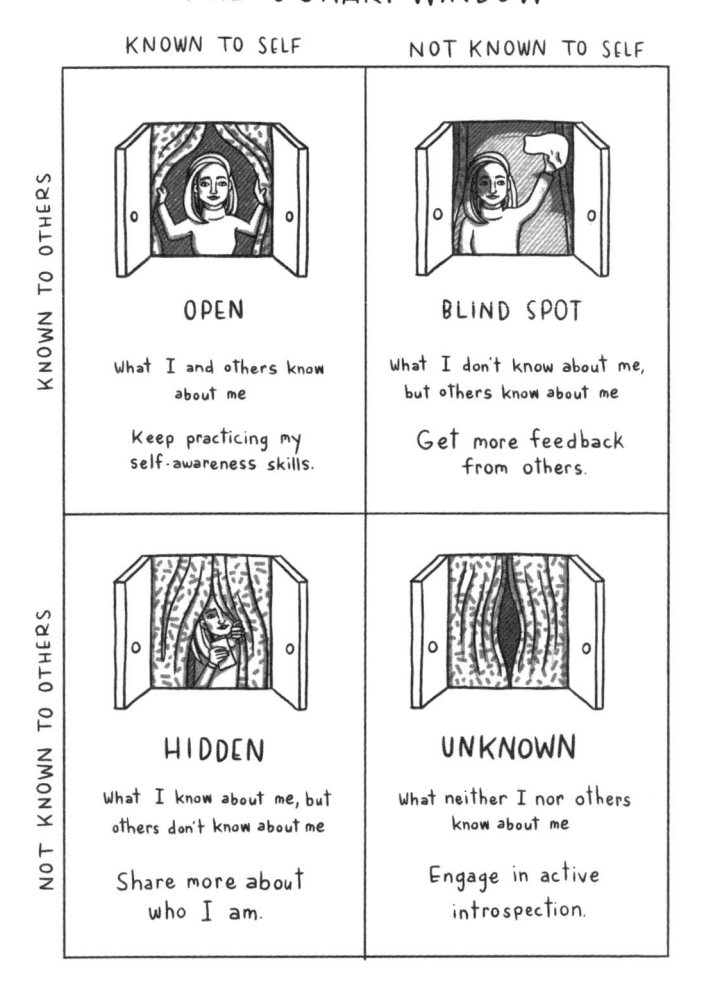

	KNOWN TO SELF	NOT KNOWN TO SELF
KNOWN TO OTHERS	**OPEN** What I and others know about me Keep practicing my self-awareness skills.	**BLIND SPOT** What I don't know about me, but others know about me Get more feedback from others.
NOT KNOWN TO OTHERS	**HIDDEN** What I know about me, but others don't know about me Share more about who I am.	**UNKNOWN** What neither I nor others know about me Engage in active introspection.

ADAPTED FROM THE JOHARI WINDOW BY PSYCHOLOGISTS JOSEPH LUFT AND HARRY INGHAM

Similarly, curiosity allows us to address the "Hidden Area or Facade." When we consciously decide to share our thoughts, feelings, or motivations with curiosity, we build bridges of trust and openness. This not only shrinks the facade but also enriches relationships by fostering mutual understanding.

Finally, the "Unknown" quadrant—those aspects of ourselves that neither we nor others can yet see—represents the ultimate domain for curiosity-driven exploration. This could include uncovering latent talents, discovering new passions, or even recognizing biases. By remaining curious about the possibilities that lie within, we expand not just our self-awareness but our capacity to connect meaningfully with others.

When we approach the Johari Window through the lens of curiosity, we begin to see it not as a static framework but as a dynamic, ever-evolving journey. In doing so, we unlock the potential for growth, understanding, and connection at every turn.

CURIOSITY DIDN'T KILL THE CAT—IT SAVED IT

Since childhood, many of us have heard the phrase "curiosity killed the cat." It's often tossed out as a cautionary warning, suggesting that too much curiosity is dangerous. But remember what you learned earlier: the full saying is actually "Curiosity killed the cat, but satisfaction brought it back," attributed to William Shakespeare, 1598.

This addition changes everything. Instead of a tale about the perils of curiosity, it becomes a story of resilience, redemption, and reward. It tells us that, while curiosity may lead us into uncertain or even risky territory, the satisfaction of exploring, learning, and discovering is what revitalizes us.

When you think about it, this expanded version of the phrase reflects the core message of this book. Curiosity—when paired with intentionality and action—leads to growth, solutions, and breakthroughs. In the workplace, curiosity encourages us to ask the questions that need to be asked, explore the opportunities others may overlook, and push through challenges to uncover what truly matters. Satisfaction doesn't come from playing it safe; it comes from taking the risks associated with curiosity and emerging stronger, wiser, and more innovative.

> The next time you hear someone say, "Curiosity killed the cat," remember to finish the phrase: "but satisfaction brought it back."

So let's rewrite how we think about curiosity. It's not a dangerous trait that needs to be tamed; it's a powerful force that drives individuals, teams, and organizations to move forward. When we embrace curiosity, we breathe new life into our ideas, our relationships, and our work. Satisfaction doesn't just bring us back; it elevates us to new heights.

The next time you hear someone say, "Curiosity killed the cat," remember to finish the phrase. Satisfaction—and the discoveries that follow—make the journey worthwhile.

What Kills Curiosity?

What's really killing our curiosity in today's fast-paced world? Here are some common culprits:

- Lack of time: When the calendar is packed, there's little room to explore, ask questions, or dive deeper.

- Fear of failure, rejection, or the unknown: "What if I'm wrong?" or "What if they judge me?" Fear can put a leash on our natural curiosity.

- Information overload: With an endless stream of news, emails, and notifications, it's hard to focus and stay curious.
- Educational factors: Sometimes, traditional systems prioritize rote learning over exploration and questioning.
- Cultural factors: Societal norms or workplace cultures that discourage challenging the status quo can stifle curiosity.
- Fatigue and stress: When you're running on empty, curiosity feels like a luxury rather than a necessity.
- Habituation and routine: Repeating the same patterns every day can make curiosity take a backseat.
- Perceived lack of relevance: "Why bother asking?" When something doesn't feel immediately useful, we may not explore it further.
- Prioritizing efficiency over exploration: In a results-driven world, we often skip the "Why" in favor of the fastest "How."

THE TAKEAWAY

Curiosity thrives when we intentionally create space for it—by questioning norms, taking risks, and giving ourselves permission to explore without judgment or fear. It's not just about asking "Why?" but also daring to follow the threads of inquiry wherever they lead, even if the answers aren't immediately clear or practical.

Overcoming the factors that kill curiosity requires a mindset shift. Instead of seeing time constraints or fear of failure as barriers, we can reframe them as challenges that curiosity helps us navigate. When we step out of routines, embrace uncertainty, and prioritize exploration over efficiency, we open ourselves to transformative growth—both personally and professionally.

Curiosity is also contagious. By modeling curiosity, whether as a leader, teammate, or friend, we inspire others to do the same. Imagine workplaces where asking questions is celebrated, where mistakes are treated as learning opportunities, and where new ideas spark innovation rather than resistance. These are the environments where curiosity truly flourishes.

It's time to reclaim our curiosity. Start small: carve out moments in your day to ask, "What if?" instead of assuming "It is what it is." Seek out experiences that challenge your comfort zone. Celebrate the discoveries you make—big or small. Every step you take to rekindle curiosity is an investment in your own potential and the future of those around you.

Let's turn the obstacles that stifle curiosity into stepping stones for opportunity, growth, and connection. After all, the more curious we are, the closer we get to a world full of possibility.

CURIOSITY AS A WAY OF LIFE

Fortunately, it's never too late to reverse direction. Curiosity isn't like a fine wine that disappears if you didn't bottle it early—it's more like that random houseplant you forgot to water for years. A little attention, some sunlight (or maybe a good TED Talk), and it'll start sprouting again. All you need is a willingness to nurture it and maybe ask a few "Why?" questions without worrying about sounding like a five-year-old. Spoiler alert: That five-year-old version of you was onto something.

The first step is to recognize the problem and commit to fostering curiosity in ourselves and others. As individuals, we can make a conscious effort to ask more questions, to seek out new experiences, and to approach challenges with a sense of wonder.

As parents and educators, we can encourage children's natural curiosity, providing them with opportunities to explore, experiment, and ask questions. We can create learning environments that value inquiry over memorization and prioritize the joy of discovery.

In the workplace, leaders can cultivate a culture of curiosity by modeling curious behavior, rewarding creative thinking, and creating space for exploration and experimentation. By fostering an environment where questions are welcomed and diverse perspectives are valued, organizations can tap into the collective wisdom of their employees and drive innovation. In the chapters to come, we look at various ways in which you can harness and develop curiosity as a skill for both personal and professional fulfillment—and how, as a leader, you can use it to shape exciting, innovative organizations where employees want to work and give their best.

Ultimately, bridging the curiosity gap requires a shift in mindset. We must recognize that curiosity is not a luxury but a necessity. In a world of rapid change and complex challenges, the ability to ask questions, learn, and adapt is not just desirable—it's essential.

As we strive to close the gap between the curiosity we have and the curiosity we need, we must remember that the journey is as important as the destination. By embracing curiosity as a way of life, we open ourselves up to a world of possibility, growth, and discovery. And that, in the end, is what it means to be truly successful.

Curiosity Reflection

Think about a time when you allowed complacency to replace curiosity. Use these prompts to reflect on how curiosity—or the lack of it—has shaped your journey:

- ☐ **Impact of complacency:** What was the effect on your decisions, relationships, or personal growth when you chose not to ask questions or explore further?

- ☐ **Missed opportunities:** What opportunities for connection, innovation, or progress might you have overlooked because curiosity wasn't part of the equation?

- ☐ **Revisiting the moment:** If you could go back to that time, what questions would you ask to gain deeper understanding or uncover new possibilities?

- ☐ **The power of curiosity:** How might approaching that situation with curiosity have changed the outcome or influenced others around you to think differently?

- ☐ **Lessons learned:** What does this reflection teach you about the role of curiosity in overcoming challenges and expanding your horizons?

Reflecting on moments like these can reveal the subtle yet transformative power of curiosity in your life. By recognizing its absence and imagining its potential, you can actively choose curiosity over routine, exploration over stagnation, and growth over staying the same. The choice to be curious is a choice to see the world—and yourself—with fresh eyes.

The Nature of Curiosity – Key Insights

- ☐ Curiosity is not a fixed trait; it is a skill that can be developed and strengthened over time.

- ☐ Environments that encourage questioning and exploration drive greater innovation and engagement.

- ☐ Curiosity signals include asking thoughtful questions, challenging assumptions, and reflecting on personal beliefs.

- ☐ Suppressing curiosity leads to stagnation and disengagement, both personally and organizationally.

- ☐ Leaders can model curiosity to foster a more open, collaborative, and innovative culture.

2
THE NEUROSCIENCE OF CURIOSITY

Five years ago, I set out to discover the link between curiosity and business performance. I was at a work session at Humana, a $117 billion healthcare company with over 100,000 employees, where I worked at the time. While another speaker was presenting, I sat next to the CEO. During a pause in the presentation, the CEO leaned over and asked, "Is curiosity innate, or can it be learned?"

And I, being the curious person I am, responded, "I don't know, but I'll look into it."

I believed then—and still believe—that curiosity is a superpower. It ignites creativity, offers a new lens for problem-solving, and serves as inner fuel for personal and professional growth. That simple question from the CEO set me on a journey of research, partnering with Lab 201 and ultimately developing the Curiosity Curve study.

Our research revealed that curiosity is indeed a skill—it can be learned and nurtured through practice. Moreover, it's contagious. The effects of curiosity can ripple through an organization, inspiring teams as they adopt these behaviors from one another. The longer someone works in a highly curious company, the more their own curiosity grows. Conversely, being in an uncurious company can stifle curiosity, leaving it to wither like a raisin in the sun.

> The longer someone works in a highly curious company, the more their own curiosity grows.

Fast forward a few weeks to my next conversation with the CEO. I shared with him, "Oh, by the way, curiosity can be learned." That simple statement shifted everything. From that moment on, I became the go-to person for all things curiosity at Humana, speaking to thousands of employees and championing the transformative power of asking questions.

In this chapter, we explore curiosity through the lens of data: how it functions in our brains, the different ways to measure it, and what optimal curiosity looks like. By understanding how curiosity applies to us as individuals, we can start thinking about how to foster it in the workplace for improved innovation and growth.

> Curiosity can be learned and nurtured through practice.

CURIOSITY ON THE BRAIN

After my conversations with the CEO of Humana, my curiosity was sparked, and I began collaborating with a group of researchers. Our purpose was to understand the link between curiosity and workplace performance, ranging from individual task completion to overall productivity and financial outcomes for the organization.

To make sense of curiosity in the workplace, we first had to define it clearly. Was it the silent intrigue of a cat, the relentless questioning of a child, the systematic pursuit of a scientist, or the strategic exploration of a business looking for an edge? We realized that understanding curiosity would require metrics based on real-world data that captured its most relevant aspects.

Despite my appreciation for data, I approached it with a healthy dose of skepticism, aware that conclusions can sometimes be misleading. For instance, correlating higher productivity with superficial changes could lead to flawed strategies or simplistic solutions that miss the complexity of what drives real performance. However, dismissing data altogether would leave us with only intuition to guide us, so we turned to neuroscience for deeper insights.

In the early 2010s, a group of London neuroscientists began studying pub trivia nights—a popular activity where people eagerly gather to test their knowledge for fun. The researchers recruited students to participate in an experiment where they answered questions they were curious about while undergoing functional magnetic resonance imaging (fMRI) scans.[1]

The fMRI machine, a large tube with sensors, measures neural activity by identifying which brain regions "light up" during specific emotions or thought processes. The researchers discovered that when participants thought about information they wanted to learn, the midbrain—also known as the mesencephalon—became active. This region, located at the top of the brainstem, is associated with essential functions like heart rate, breathing, and sleep and is closely linked to areas of the brain involved in desire and motivation.

However, the midbrain doesn't work alone. For true learning and retention, it collaborates with the hippocampus, the brain's memory and learning center. This region plays a key role in both short-term and long-term memory. The secret to harnessing curiosity is engaging the hippocampus to work with the midbrain. When these regions "reconnect" and engage in learning together, individuals can challenge outdated assumptions, unlearn stale information, and rewire their thinking with new insights that fuel personal and professional growth.

Another key player in the neuroscience of curiosity is the nucleus accumbens, the brain's reward center. This region activates when we anticipate a positive experience, such as receiving a gift or completing a task. It's also integral to learning associations between actions and outcomes, famously studied by Ivan Pavlov in his experiments with dogs. The role of the nucleus accumbens in curiosity suggests that the pursuit of knowledge is motivated by the expectation of a reward. When we encounter new, intriguing information, our brains release pleasurable dopamine, reinforcing the behavior and encouraging further exploration.

The interplay of the midbrain, hippocampus, and nucleus accumbens paints a compelling picture of how curiosity works in the brain. Beyond this, research from institutions like MIT is uncovering potential links between cognitive resilience and the prevention of certain types of dementia. Activities that cultivate curiosity—such as puzzles, reading, or social engagement—appear to strengthen these brain functions, suggesting that curiosity could be a protective factor against cognitive decline.[2]

Clearly, practicing curiosity enhances human capability. With this understanding, we turned our attention to exploring how these neurological insights could translate into organizational performance and culture.

I SEEK, I EXPLORE, I FEEL DEPRIVED

One way to study curiosity is to ask people what they do and how they do it. Survey instruments are a common tool in social science research. Though researchers have studied a wide range of personality traits like extroversion, curiosity research didn't gain momentum until the early 2000s. Three measures of curiosity stood out from the pack: epistemic curiosity, deprivation, and curiosity and exploration.

Epistemic simply means "related to knowledge." The epistemic curiosity, or EC, scale focuses on the positive feelings associated with gaining intellectual knowledge, such as learning new ideas and understanding how things work. The EC scale taps into the inherent joy and excitement that comes from satisfying one's curiosity about the world. Developed by Jordan Litman and Charles Spielberger in 2003 at the University of South Florida, it has become one of the most influential measurement tools in the field, probably because it's so optimistic and encouraging about people.[3]

The Epistemic Curiosity Scale

The EC scale uses 10 items to measure curiosity:

- ☐ I enjoy learning about subjects that are unfamiliar.

- ☐ It is fascinating to learn new information.

- ☐ I enjoy exploring new ideas.

- ☐ When learning about something new, I like to find out more.

- ☐ I enjoy discussing abstract concepts.

- ☐ When I see a complicated piece of machinery, I ask someone how it works.

- ☐ When faced with new kinds of arithmetic problems, I enjoy imagining solutions.

- ☐ When I see an incomplete puzzle, I try and imagine the final solution.

- ☐ I am interested in discovering how things work.

- ☐ When I hear a riddle, I am interested in trying to solve it.

Another measure takes the opposite approach. It looks at curiosity as a nuisance or an annoyance. Sometimes the desire to know can be driven by a sense of unease or tension, a feeling that something is missing or incomplete. This negative view is captured by the curiosity as a feeling of deprivation (CFD) scale, developed by Litman and Tiffany Jimerson, also at the University of South Florida, in 2004.[4]

Like the EC scale, the CFD scale assesses the desire to obtain intellectual knowledge unrelated to people, such as facts and problem-solving skills. However, the CFD scale emphasizes the discomfort and irritation associated with having your curiosity thwarted or unsatisfied.

Imagine the frustration of having a word or phrase on the tip of your tongue, just out of reach. The CFD scale asks about the intensity of this negative feeling, providing a window into the more challenging aspects of curiosity.

A third metric looks at the experience of wanting to know and flow. The curiosity and exploration inventory (CEI), developed in 2004 by Todd Kashdan, Paul Rose, and Frank Fincham at the State University of New York at Buffalo, was designed to quantify that experience.[5]

The CEI asks people about two key dimensions of curiosity: exploration and absorption. Exploration, in this context, means striving for novelty and challenge, the desire to seek out new experiences and push oneself beyond one's comfort zone. Absorption, on the other hand, refers to the state of full engagement in specific activities, the experience of being "in the zone" or "in flow." By assessing these two dimensions, the CEI captures the dynamic, experiential aspects of curiosity that go beyond simply being interested in acquiring information.

The Curiosity and Exploration Inventory

In the CEI, researchers ask the following questions:

- ☐ I would describe myself as someone who actively seeks as much information as I can in a new situation.

- ☐ When I am participating in an activity, I tend to get so involved that I lose track of time.

- ☐ I frequently find myself looking for new opportunities to grow as a person (e.g., information, people, resources).

- ☐ I am not the type of person who probes deeply into new situations or things.

- ☐ When I am actively interested in something, it takes a great deal to interrupt me.

- ☐ My friends would describe me as someone who is "extremely intense" when in the middle of doing something.

- ☐ Everywhere I go, I am out looking for new things or experiences.

We seek knowledge. We explore our world. And we feel deprived when we are frustrated by not being able to learn what we want to learn. Taken together, these three measurement approaches provide a picture of curiosity in all its complexity. They highlight the positive and negative emotions associated with curiosity, as well as the behavioral and experiential dimensions of exploration and engagement.

OPTIMAL CURIOSITY

For hundreds of years, great minds like Plato, Socrates, and Descartes have searched for the secret of achievement. What makes one person achieve success and another not?

The answer may involve optimal curiosity. Not too little—but also not too much.

I love my friend Elizabeth—and she also drives me crazy. Whenever we talk, she'll wonder about what's going to happen in politics, and then about how to solve the healthcare crisis, and what is going to happen next in global culture, and the possibilities for scientific breakthroughs or inflation. I can usually keep up with her for an hour or so, but after a while, I want to say, "Can we just talk about *The Real Housewives of Beverly Hills*?"

My brain fills up faster than hers. She raises too many ideas, and many of them are problems that somebody should deal with. But there are too many to contemplate. It would take too much attention. And there's only so much time in a day.

Fortunately, Elizabeth and I have the kind of relationship where I can say, "Okay, we need to shift here. Let's stop solving the world's problems." There are leaders like Elizabeth who run large companies, and if left unchecked, I can easily imagine that their teams might feel intimidated, leading to two common responses: Either they grit their teeth and endure it, or they disengage completely. Curiosity exists on a delicate continuum—too much, and we're overwhelmed; too little, and innovation grinds to a halt. Striking the right balance is what drives progress and keeps teams thriving.

I've had to learn this lesson. I was once hired from outside a company to take over a team when its leader left. In the first meeting, we went around, and everyone described their roles. I responded to each person with enthusiastic questions and ideas about how to win new business. It felt like brainstorming; I thought I was breaking the ice. It was inspired by the possibilities.

The next day, the finance proposal team called me in a panic. My new direct reports had come in that morning and immediately started executing most of what I'd talked about. I had thought it was an ideation session where I could find out what they were thinking and where they could satisfy their curiosity about me. But they thought I was telling them what to do. I had overestimated their curiosity level.

After that, I recognized that curiosity has consequences. When you're a boss, at any level, people will assume you mean business when you come up with an idea. You have to think before you speak and deliberately explain when you're brainstorming versus when you're making a direct command. Otherwise, curiosity dissolves into confusion.

There is *optimal* curiosity, in other words: not too little and not too much.

Curiosity is not an unalloyed good. The curiosity expressed by an individual employee or manager has a different effect than the curiosity expressed by an organization. People with the highest curiosity levels tend to score high on engagement and job satisfaction—but not all the time and not consistently.

In Figure 2.1, for example, we see the curiosity and exploration inventory (CEI) introduced earlier, here charted against job satisfaction. This measure was taken for the same group of 313 employed adults we evaluated in Figure 1.1 and divided them into groups according to their individual curiosity levels, ranked from 1 (lowest curiosity) to 8 (highest).

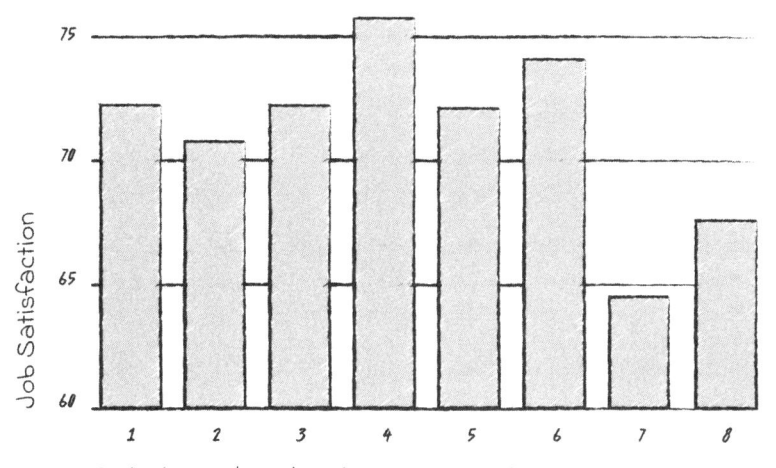

Figure 2.1: Optimal curiosity levels for job satisfaction
Source: Lab 201, Curiosity Curve survey, 2023

The low-curious to somewhat-curious groups (groups 1 through 6) have roughly similar levels of job satisfaction, mostly within 3 percentage points. There's a slight peak for the mid-curious group 4.

Then notice the two most-curious groups: 7 and 8. They're a full 7 to 9 percentage points below the others. In job satisfaction that's a significant drop, and this difference represents a major shift in attitude. Those with the highest individual curiosity scores show the least job satisfaction—and may even be ready to quit.

What does this suggest to you? To our researchers, it suggests that there is an optimal level of curiosity for individual decision-makers in an organization: Too little curiosity leads them to stagnate, while too much leads them to distraction and frustration.

That optimal level of curiosity varies from one company to the next. It may also vary by individual or across the course of a career. We therefore need to learn to find the optimal curiosity setpoint for ourselves and our organizations. When we exceed that setpoint, driven forward by our curiosity, we need to pay attention to our choices. We may be about to reach a breakthrough—or we may be in danger of getting fired.

You may think that curiosity is worth the price of risking your job. Many people do. Even so, the choice of leaving should be deliberate and conscious. If you want to stay, or if you aren't sure, then you may need to manage your curiosity more effectively.

Managing curiosity is difficult because it is closely tied to emotion. People feel drawn to the intrinsic joy of exploring something new. We feel a sensation of pleasure when our questions are answered, and as we've seen with the curiosity as a feeling of deprivation scale, we feel disappointed when our curiosity is unsatisfied.

THE CULTURAL CURIOSITY SCALE

These curiosity metrics all assess *individuals*, but they have limited value for organizations trying to raise their performance. They don't measure curiosity as it relates to an organization's culture, and they don't quite capture the complex interplay between the employee and the organizational context—particularly its approach to exploration and learning.

So Cory Kim, founder of the research group Lab 201, and I created our own. Called the Cultural Curiosity Scale (CCS), it revealed some issues we would never have understood otherwise.

We started by conducting a comprehensive review of existing scales—the EC, CEI, and CFD among them—on various aspects of organizational curiosity, individual curiosity, management style, and organizational values. We looked for common themes and key dimensions that could inform the development of a new instrument.

Based on this analysis, we crafted a set of survey questions designed to probe employees' perceptions of their organization's culture of curiosity. Rather than asking individuals to rate their own curiosity, the questions focused on behaviors and practices that reflect an organization's commitment to exploration, learning, and innovation.

The Cultural Curiosity Scale

For the CCS, we designed an instrument that identifies individual expressions of curiosity within a cultural environment as well as the ability of the cultural environment to allow and nurture these expressions of curiosity. To identify these individual expressions of curiosity, the CCS includes such items as:

- ☐ Even when I am confident in my approach to a problem, I like to hear other people's opinions.

- ☐ When a complex work problem arises, I continue to ask questions until I understand it fully.

In assessing environmental factors, the CCS includes such items as:

- ☐ In discussions and meetings, I am encouraged and enabled to ask questions.

- ☐ I am encouraged to try out new ideas or approaches without fear of negative consequences.

- ☐ My opinions seem to count.

We then recruited a diverse sample of 313 working adults from a range of industries and demographic backgrounds. They completed an online survey that included our new CCS, as well as established measures of individual curiosity, job satisfaction, and willingness to recommend their workplace to others.

We put the CCS through a rigorous series of statistical tests to assess its reliability, validity, and predictive power. Then we conducted regression analyses to optimize the scale's ability to estimate an organization's underlying curiosity values.

The results were promising. The CCS demonstrated high internal consistency and complemented the validity of other established instruments. Importantly, the scale also diverged from previous measures of individual curiosity in a way that suggests that this metric captures something unique about the organizational climate for curiosity.[6]

Of course, no study is without limitations. But when we looked at the data, we found it was consistent with the findings of other research in the field and with our own experience. Moreover, by every metric we found, curiosity is good for business—which is what we delve into more deeply in the next chapter.

Curiosity Reflection

How did your curiosity impact the people around you, particularly those you lead or influence?

- ☐ Did you notice any hesitation or frustration from others in response to your ideas or questions?

- ☐ If you could revisit that moment, how would you balance curiosity with clarity to create a more focused dialogue?

- ☐ What approaches could you use to communicate curiosity without overwhelming others?

How did heightened curiosity affect your engagement and job satisfaction?

- ☐ What were the key moments when your curiosity may have driven you away from feeling content or stable?

- ☐ If you could approach that experience differently, how might you have managed your curiosity to foster a more satisfying outcome?

- ☐ What signs can you look for in the future to gauge when curiosity is becoming counterproductive?

How did your curiosity-driven ideas or brainstorming affect your team or colleagues' perception of your intent?

- ☐ What were the consequences when curiosity wasn't clearly framed as ideation versus directive?

- ☐ How might framing curiosity differently have clarified your expectations and reduced misunderstandings?

- ☐ What steps can you take to communicate your curiosity in ways that invite open feedback?

How did your curiosity align (or not align) with your organization's values around exploration and innovation?

- ☐ What was the reaction from others, and how did it influence your engagement or approach?

- ☐ If you could revisit this moment, what questions might you ask to gain insight into your organization's cultural curiosity?

- ☐ How could you support a culture of curiosity that balances innovation with organizational stability?

How did your curiosity for exploring options impact the timeliness and clarity of your decision?

- ☐ What was the effect of this approach on your confidence in the outcome?

- ☐ Looking back, what questions could you have asked to bring focus and avoid distraction?

- ☐ How might curiosity have served you better by prompting a deeper look at fewer choices?

How did achieving a balance of curiosity impact your sense of job satisfaction or engagement?

- ☐ What specific actions helped you achieve the right amount of curiosity without tipping into distraction?

- ☐ If you could draw on this experience in other areas, what practices might you carry forward to maintain an optimal level of curiosity?

- ☐ How has finding this balance influenced those around you and set a tone for sustainable curiosity?

3
CURIOSITY IS GOOD BUSINESS

I wasn't surprised to find that curiosity is good for business. As an employee, a business leader, and a consultant, I have seen the value of curiosity in action. Moreover, at the start of my career, I had spent nearly a decade working for one of the most innovative and curious companies in the world.

Frito-Lay, a division of PepsiCo, has long been renowned for its ability to listen to customers and introduce popular new snacks. It also invented the handheld computer as a device used by its distribution route drivers to track stock flow.[1] So yes, I was fortunate to be there. I learned more about curiosity there than at any other company. That experience, in which I rose from being a route driver in the city of Detroit to a marketing executive, taught me that curiosity in a company is not a matter of the top executives. Every person in a company is a link in a chain of intrigue.

At least, that's the way it's supposed to be. In real life, even the most innovative companies, like Frito-Lay, don't fully know how to cultivate the curiosity they need all the way through the hierarchy.

CURIOSITY IN THE CORN CHIP AISLE

When I went to work at Frito-Lay fresh from business school, driving my route truck and delivering snacks was a physically demanding job. Every morning at 4 a.m., I showed up at the warehouse to load the truck. Fritos. Doritos. Ruffles. Cheetos. Funyuns. Rold Gold pretzels. Then, all day, I would pop and lace. "Popping and lacing" was a Frito-Lay term. It described their preferred way to put the snacks on a rack to make them look irresistible. It was my specialty—and I still take great pride in it. To this day, no snack rack is safe from my prowess. A few minutes after I walk into a Piggly Wiggly, the manager of the store is likely to say over the intercom: "Ma'am? Step away from the rack."

It wasn't always easy at Frito-Lay. Take Hank, the warehouse manager—he just didn't care for me. No reason, really. Maybe I'd grumbled once about standing in line to load my truck. Or possibly I'd dented a truck or two (three, tops). But whatever the reason, Hank had it out for me.

One Friday afternoon, I was in the breakroom filling out my weekly paperwork when I suddenly heard his voice bellowing from the dock. "Clary, get out here!" The heads of my fellow route drivers popped up in curiosity as I sheepishly made my way over to Hank, who was standing there, hands on his hips, right in front of a route truck. His eyes zeroed in on me, and then, with a dramatic flair, he pointed to the tires.

"Do you see the damage to these tires? I could fire you right now for destroying company property. No write-up, no warning, no union representation—just fired. You are so careless."

I nodded, playing along. "I see what you mean, Hank. That does look pretty bad."

He leaned in, giving me that "gotcha" glare. "So, Clary, what do you have to say for yourself?"

"Me? Oh . . . that's not my truck, Hank."

The color drained from his face as he glanced around, catching the amused looks from the other drivers. His credibility, just like that, was punctured. If only Hank had asked, "Is this your truck?" he could have saved himself the embarrassment. That day, I learned the power of a question: It can make or break a moment.

That encounter with Hank was a perfect illustration of the power of a question. It's something I've seen time and again in my career—questions shape the course of conversations, decisions, and even reputations. They can reveal hidden truths, build bridges, and open doors to unexpected insights. But they also hold the power to unravel carefully constructed moments when they're not asked.

A single question, like "Is this your truck?" would have shifted the entire interaction between Hank and me. It would have signaled curiosity rather than assumption, a desire to understand before reacting. Questions are unique in that they don't just communicate; they invite. They create space for dialogue, an openness that assumptions close off.

In leadership, the power of a question is invaluable. The best leaders I've known use questions as their most powerful tool—not because they lack answers but because they value the responses of others. They know that one good question can unlock an idea that transforms a project, spark a connection that strengthens a team, or prevent a misstep that could cost time, resources, or credibility.

Looking back, I've come to realize that questions are often more potent than statements, especially when things get heated. A question invites the other person to clarify, to open up, to contribute something that wasn't previously on the table. "What's your take on this?" "How could we approach this differently?" "What am I missing here?" These questions signal respect, encourage collaboration, and help us see the world through someone else's eyes. It's a small act that can have a monumental impact.

In contrast, not asking the right question—or jumping to conclusions—often builds walls instead of bridges. When Hank chose accusation over inquiry, he created a distance between us. Rather than building my respect, he ended up with an embarrassing lesson in front of his team. This taught me that when we lead with questions, we lead with humility, curiosity, and a willingness to understand.

For anyone who wants to influence, inspire, or connect, questions are one of the most potent tools we have. It's not always about having the answer; often, the most transformative moments come from asking the right question.

The delivery work was decent for a young woman in her early twenties, but it came with its fair share of frustrations. One recurring irritation? Male store managers who'd ask if I was "still Free-to-Lay." The joke was stale long before I'd heard it.

The job had its hazards, too. We carried cash. I was only robbed once, and I attribute that safety record to a mix of rude resilience and the company's self-defense training program. Frito-Lay taught us to scare off threats by staying a step ahead, ready for anything. The mantra was simple: Stay ahead of the situation.

Unfortunately, the self-defense training didn't work wonders for my dating life. One tactic was to use hardcore profanity to startle potential thieves—especially when it came from a woman. But as a Southern Baptist, I couldn't bring myself to drop a string of curses. Instead, I'd call out "Don't come any closer, mother ducker! Trust me, you don't want a piece of this." Not quite as intimidating as intended, but it got the job done.

Despite these obstacles, I excelled at my job. When the Frito-Lay bigwigs came in from Dallas, my route was chosen for inspection. Within nine months, I'd earned a promotion to district sales manager at 25, and by 27, I was regional sales manager with a new vantage point on the company. From a few rungs higher, I started to understand some of the challenges I'd faced on the route. The real issue was simple yet profound: Organizations are made up of people, and people are unpredictable. They show up one day, disappear the next, and sometimes keep secrets.

One young driver was known as Good Guy Joe. He was reliable and performed well, but we noticed discrepancies in his paperwork. His sales didn't match his inventory, and nobody could make sense of it. My bosses wanted him gone, but I wasn't convinced. I asked to talk to Joe first. I brought him into my office, and as soon as I asked him what was going on, he opened up in a way that told me he hadn't had a chance to explain this to anyone who'd listen.

"Miss Debbie," he began, "I'll give it to you straight. You know Pauly down at the Wawa?" (Wawa is a major convenience store chain, and at the time, it was struggling against an influx of new competitors.) "Well, I noticed Pauly looked stressed, so I asked him how he was doing." (Many of the franchisees were dealing with tight cash flows, and Pauly was no exception.)

"We've had his business for years, and I know you wouldn't want to lose him. So I gave him a promotional price early to help him stay competitive. I promise I wasn't stealing anything."

In just a few minutes, Joe had revealed an intricate strategy that helped the customer, the company, and, yes, his sales numbers. He had technically broken the rules, but he wasn't stealing. He was curious and willing to step out of line to keep our business strong. That conversation changed things: Instead of firing him, Frito-Lay created a new policy based on his approach, allowing flexible promotional pricing to benefit customers like Pauly. I learned that curiosity isn't just a path to problem-solving; it's a signal to people like Joe that their voices matter.

> Companies that don't value curiosity often overlook their best ideas.

This experience demonstrated the many ways a lack of curiosity can harm a business's bottom line. Companies that don't value curiosity often overlook their best ideas, alienate their most dedicated employees, and misread their customers' needs. I've heard it said that the employees with the most customer information are the least consulted—and it's true. Had Joe's insight been ignored, Frito-Lay might have lost Pauly's business.

I still consider Frito-Lay one of the best companies, not only because they promoted me but because they recognized Joe's value and rewarded his intuition. Not every company would do that, but there's always room to expand curiosity. The power of inquiry is a force for improvement.

In the rest of this chapter, we explore the benefits of fostering continuous curiosity in the business world.

> In the CCS research conducted with Lab 201, we created a scale to measure curiosity as a cultural value against performance indicators. The findings revealed three major benefits of a curious culture: more successful innovation, higher job satisfaction and employee engagement, and longer employee tenure.

Curiosity, it turns out, is not only a virtue but a competitive advantage.

ONLY THE CURIOUS INNOVATE

Innovation is the ability to put forth new ideas and turn them into successful products, services, and practices, leading to profits and growth. Organizations with curious cultures tend to attract and retain curious individuals. This creates a virtuous cycle where curious minds feed off each other, fostering an environment that encourages exploration and experimentation. When employees feel empowered to ask questions, challenge assumptions, and propose new ideas, they are more likely to uncover novel solutions and create new products and services. This works especially well when teams bring together divergent thinkers who are curious about one another's backgrounds and knowledge.

> Organizations that foster curiosity turn potential loss into growth and productivity.

Several studies have replicated the positive relationship between individual curiosity and organizational innovation. One study asked 480 corporate employees holding 188 different jobs about the way they thought at work. They found that people with higher levels of curiosity tend to exhibit stronger innovation skills, especially around ideation.[2] Another study, involving American and German employees, linked some of the curiosity scores I mentioned in Chapter 2, such as exploration and the feeling of deprivation, to successful innovation.[3] Merck set up a Curiosity Council that published a book about the correlation; it's called *Curious2018: Future Insights in Science and Technology.*[4]

Entrepreneurs are curious people by nature. This quality extends to university students. A 2018 study on college students starting new businesses found a significant positive correlation between curiosity, self-efficacy, and innovative behavior. Intrinsic motivation matters.[5]

Individual curiosity, however, is not enough to spark widespread innovation in an enterprise. It also requires a high level of organizational support. I've seen many organizations bring in a so-called big thinker in a field like digital analytics and expect that individual to drive change. In many cases, the new approach doesn't take, the rest of the organization ignores them, and they ultimately leave without making any of the expected impact. They were hired to be different, and they are run out of the company because they're different.

The solution is to find them a place to land where they can demonstrate results and gradually influence the rest of the organization. Art Kleiner, former editor of PwC's magazine *strategy+business*, said that he worked with many innovators at that large professional services firm because people with innate curiosity tended to write articles.

In his five years there, however, he saw many of those innovators struggle to gain support. The people who stayed were those who found a base of support: an institute within PwC, a regular series of workshops, or a consulting practice in a particular field like AI. Those who needed to justify their value each time, even if they were lucrative contributors, often got frustrated and left.[6]

CURIOUS COMPANIES EARN COMMITMENT

Companies spend countless hours and resources trying to crack the code on how to keep their employees motivated, productive, and committed. But what if the answer lies not in trendy perks or even incentives but in something far more personal? What if the key to unlocking employee engagement is fostering a culture of curiosity?

In the research I completed with Lab 201 for this book (December 2022), a staggering 93% of employees in companies with highly curious cultures reported being engaged in their work, compared to a mere 47% in companies with low curiosity scores. That's a difference of nearly 50 percentage points. Employees in highly curious companies are also more likely to rate their managers and leaders more highly on leadership practices (87% versus 38%).

Moreover, curious cultures foster collaboration and knowledge-sharing among employees. When individuals are curious about each other's experiences and expertise, they are more likely to reach out, connect, and work together toward common goals. This creates a virtuous cycle of engagement, where employees feel valued for their contributions and are inspired to give their best effort.

Curiosity also enables resilience. Individuals and teams who are genuinely curious about changing circumstances and market conditions are more likely to find ways to manage them.

But perhaps the most compelling argument for the power of curiosity in driving engagement lies in the stark contrast between companies that prioritize it and those that don't. In organizations with average levels on our Cultural Curiosity Scale (CCS), 73% of employees report being satisfied with their jobs, 50% would recommend their workplace to others, and the average tenure is five years. While these numbers are respectable, they pale in comparison to the 90% job satisfaction, 71% recommendation rate, and six-year average tenure seen in highly curious companies.

Figure 3.1 illustrates this correlation by mapping CCS scores against key engagement metrics—job satisfaction, workplace recommendations, and employee tenure. The data makes a clear case: As curiosity levels rise, so does engagement. Employees in highly curious workplaces feel a stronger sense of purpose, greater alignment with leadership, and a deeper connection to their work. In contrast, companies with low curiosity scores struggle with lower engagement, reduced job satisfaction, and higher turnover.

In short, the more curious your company, the more likely employees are to feel in sync with their leaders, their work, and the broader mission of the organization. Figure 3.1 provides a visual representation of this dynamic, reinforcing how curiosity isn't just a cultural nicety—it's a strategic advantage.

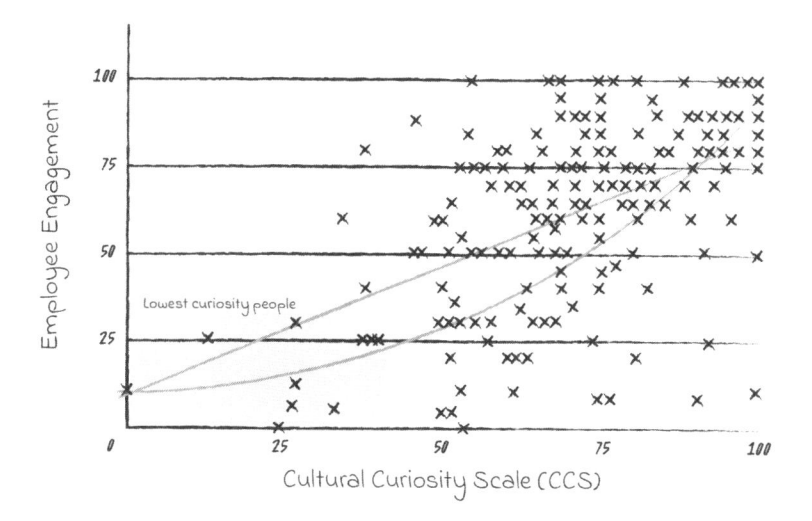

Figure 3.1: A Curiosity Curve for
culture and employee engagement

Source: Lab 201, Curiosity Curve survey, 2023

The converse is also true. Look at the engagement scores for people working in cultures with low curiosity. *No one* feels any sense of engagement higher than 30%. They're all in the light gray box at the bottom left, which seems like a grim place to be. With that low level of engagement, the place they work probably bores them—or worse, is a source of high stress or pain. (Some high-curiosity people also feel this way, which probably means they are mismatched with their employer.) The lower areas are relatively sparse, probably because people working in these cultures tend to leave.

I spent nearly a decade in a marketing team at Coca-Cola that reminds me of the lower levels on this chart. I was chief of staff to a senior vice president named Tony. He had a tendency to think and speak at the same time. I hadn't noticed this when we first started working together, but I soon learned that it was standard practice. Tony would ask me to do something. I'd expend an extraordinary amount of effort researching the idea, writing a marketing plan and financial budget, and detailing the resources required to execute it. Feeling very proud of myself, I'd share it with Tony, and he would say, "I've thought of something else."

After a few months of frustration, I checked in with my predecessor as chief of staff. "If he asks for something once, ignore it," she counseled me. "If he asks a second time, ignore it. If he asks a third time, take action."

The message is clear: If companies want to unlock the full potential of their workforce, it's not enough to hire curious individuals. They need to create a culture that values and rewards exploration, learning, and innovation. This takes commitment. Employees will want to ask questions, explore new ideas, and challenge conventional wisdom. The organization must promote leaders who embody and champion those behaviors—at least to some extent.

The next step is to look more closely at your organization in particular to see what kind of curiosity level is optimal for you.

EMPLOYEES IN CURIOUS CULTURES STICK AROUND

Companies often overlook a critical factor that can make or break their ability to attract and keep top talent: the curiosity of their culture. When leaders are complacent, they're essentially saying to their employees, "Nothing can touch us, and we don't want to hear about problems. Not only are we not curious about them, but if someone raises questions, we don't pay attention. We're strong enough to cover the issue."

Companies with that attitude are often unable or unwilling to adapt to changing circumstances. Gatekeepers inside the organization may dismiss new ideas out of hand, preferring to stick with the status quo even in the face of mounting evidence that change is necessary. In such an environment, employees who raise questions or challenge established ways of thinking may be met with resistance or even hostility. Leaders who propose new ideas will be met with polite lip service or ignored.

As curiosity increases and the curve gets higher, so does performance. Innovation levels rise. Products are not just conceptualized but actually launched. Individual performance metrics go up on average, and so do job satisfaction rates. People in companies with higher curiosity report longer tenure in their roles, and in general, turnover is relatively low.

We found a similarly strong correlation between cultural curiosity and employee retention. Take a look at Figure 3.2. Organizations that cultivate a culture of questioning, exploration, and continuous learning appear to be more likely to keep their employees for the long haul. Retention rates are a whopping 80% for individuals in the top 10% of curious cultures, compared to a mere 40% for those in the bottom 10%.

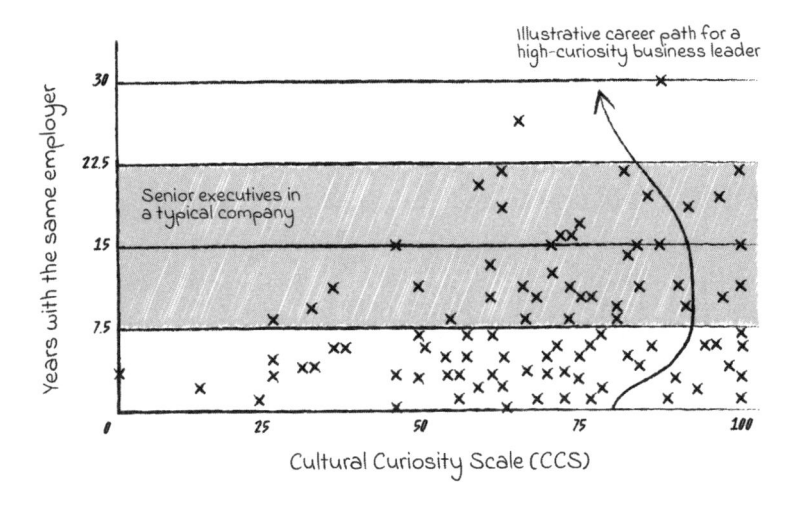

Figure 3.2: Cultural curiosity and job tenure

Source: Lab 201, Curiosity Curve survey, 2023

We have to be careful with job tenure data. For instance, if people have only been in their jobs a year, that doesn't mean they're going to leave; they might end up staying in place for years. In our research, we did not find much correlation between job retention and any of the individual curiosity scores, such as epistemic curiosity, curiosity as a feeling of deprivation, or the curiosity and exploration inventory. The retention rates vary so much among these measures for the same group of people that we're tempted to believe there is no relationship. A person with high curiosity might stay in their position for 2 years, 10 years, or 30.

By contrast, the correlation between a curious culture and longer job tenure is robust. Employees in curious cultures tend to stick around. Indeed, cultural curiosity is a better predictor of retention than anything else we've seen—including job satisfaction levels and the track record of promotions and salary increases. Since high job turnover is often devastating to a company, this is a significant finding. It's especially pronounced for people who have been in place seven years or more, which makes it even more robust because it reduces the statistical noise of people who left for other reasons.

This finding reminds us that a corporate culture is not the average consensus of the views within it. As an individual, you can believe very strongly about something while working within a culture that follows a different perspective. Your beliefs may not change, but your behavior, to some extent, will align with that of the organization. Otherwise, you won't last there very long. So you may compartmentalize—leaving behind your values, at least to some extent, when you walk in the company door.

In Figure 3.2, the curved line with an arrow shows what an individual career path might look like. When you first join a company, you tend to be naturally curious—especially if you're fresh out of school and it's your first job. Ideally, your curiosity turns out to match well with your workplace: Your boss and your colleagues encourage you to keep an open mind and explore new things. In this case, you've found an optimal curiosity level, so you stay in place. You continually get new challenges, and you are inventive and innovative enough to manage them. You get promoted. Meanwhile, your peers are either more curious or less curious than you. They leave for other places that represent a better match.

By your 15-year point, you may be a leader at that organization. Your high curiosity has been rewarded.

But maybe after 22 years, you've been there so long that you've become a bit complacent. Your score slips down—just a little. Maybe you find yourself just waiting for the time you can retire.

Ultimately, there's a lesson here for CEOs and other top corporate leaders: If you want high retention and all the benefits that go with it, then cultivate curiosity. Pay particular attention to people within the light gray box in Figure 3.2: those who have lasted at your company for 7.5 years or more. These tend to be critically important managers and employees because they mentor others. Their curiosity levels tend to be high as a group, which suggests that curiosity spreads infectiously in their companies.

If curiosity is contagious, these people are the viral influencers in the workplace. Help them understand their value and the need to mentor others. Give them opportunities to exercise their curiosity on behalf of the company. Learn from their failures as well as their successes. Make sure they are seen, their opinions are heard, and they are drawn into strategy. One of them may be your successor. All of them are ready to amplify your company's strategy.

When individuals feel encouraged to ask questions, challenge assumptions, and seek out new knowledge, they experience a greater sense of purpose and fulfillment in their work. They feel valued for their contributions and are more likely to stay engaged and committed. This is especially true if they have colleagues and bosses with similar levels of curiosity. The conversations in the break room, after work, or on a Zoom call take on their own value. All of that makes it easier for these curious viral influencers to stay at a company, especially if their creativity and energy lead them to promotions.

The Curiosity Setpoint

Curiosity exists on a continuum. While too little curiosity can stifle creativity and hinder progress, an overly curious culture can lead to endless ideation without practical outcomes, creating distractions that can even affect profitability. The key is finding a balance—what we call the *curiosity setpoint*. This setpoint represents the optimal level of curiosity within an organization where exploration is encouraged but channeled productively, ensuring ideas are translated into actionable outcomes rather than becoming endless speculation.

As we saw in the introduction, curiosity and exploration inventory (CEI) scores correlate with job satisfaction—but only up to a certain level. This correlation indicates that there is an ideal point at which curiosity drives engagement without detracting from focus or stability. Figure 3.3 shows a similar pattern for job tenure in relation to curiosity as a feeling of deprivation (CFD) scores. These scores reflect people who feel an uncomfortable need to satisfy their curiosity. Interestingly, those likely to stay with a company the longest exhibit moderate curiosity levels—an indication of the curiosity setpoint for this group of organizations.

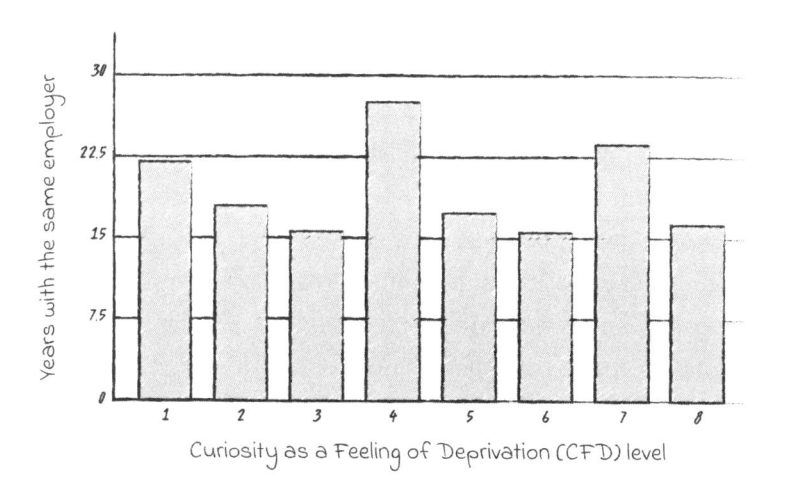

Figure 3.3: The curiosity setpoint

Source: Lab 201, Curiosity Curve survey, 2023

The chart also illustrates that the curiosity levels of people who have been with their company for over 20 years vary widely. Group 1, for example, represents those with very low curiosity levels, while Group 4 appears to have reached a balanced level—moderate curiosity that is neither too low nor too high. Meanwhile, Group 7 members, even after two decades, display strong curiosity, eager to explore new ideas and opportunities. This ranking, from low to high curiosity, helps clarify where individuals fall along the curiosity continuum.

The data suggest that finding your optimal curiosity level—the curiosity setpoint—may depend on aligning with your company's culture rather than relying solely on personal habits or natural inclination. Employees with a curiosity level that complements their organization's environment tend to stay longer, suggesting that leaders should aim to foster a level of curiosity that encourages exploration while aligning with organizational goals.

Companies that neglect curiosity risk losing their most energetic and innovative talent. Yet those with hypercurious cultures, where every question triggers dozens more and each brainstorming session spawns multiple projects, may create environments of perpetual distraction. When leaders introduce a constant flow of new ideas without setting clear priorities, they offload their curiosity burden onto their teams, leaving employees uncertain about where to focus their time and energy. Finding a curiosity setpoint that balances innovation with direction is crucial for sustaining meaningful progress.

FINDING THE OPTIMAL LEVEL

The key, then, is to find the optimal level of curiosity—the sweet spot on the curve where curiosity drives innovation without tipping over into chaos. One way to do this is to think about clarity. Cultivate purposeful curiosity, where the pursuit of new ideas is balanced with a commitment to making informed decisions and taking decisive action.

Some studies have suggested ways to do this. One example is the Innovation 1000, a study that originated at Booz Allen Hamilton and then its spinoff Booz & Company. For 10 years, between 2005 and 2015, a team led by consultant Barry Jaruzelski analyzed the 1,000 companies around the world that spent the most on research and development. They consistently found no statistically significant relationship between sustained financial performance and research and development (R&D) spending, either in total dollars or as a percentage of revenues. Some companies with large R&D budgets put out fewer successful products than similar companies with smaller budgets.[7]

So Jaruzelski began to look at what made the difference. It wasn't just curiosity. In fact, after a certain level, curiosity simply led people to follow their ideas in multiple scattered directions, with no sustained improvement. The most successful innovators were what Jaruzelski and his coauthors called *Need Seekers*, because they took their priorities from their customers.

According to Jaruzelski, companies like Apple, Procter & Gamble, and Tesla gain competitive advantage by directly engaging customers to uncover unstated future needs. They prioritize insights from customer interactions, big data, and industry trends, fostering a culture of openness to new ideas that drives innovation and enterprise-wide product launches.

I've often heard executives debate how much revenue should be spent on R&D or innovation. Others debate how much should be spent on learning and development, at least in terms of best practices. The focus on investment is itself a distraction.

Curiosity, in itself, doesn't cost anything. The investment begins when you implement your decisions and designs.

The most prudent, effective approach is to become deliberate about the curiosity in your company. Now that we've immersed ourselves in some of the data on curiosity and seen how it makes a difference in terms of employee satisfaction and longevity, we'll get more specific about the growth factors of curious companies—and what you can do to inspire curiosity in yours.

Curiosity Reflection

Think of a time when you felt aligned with your organization's level of curiosity:

- ☐ How did this alignment impact your engagement and job satisfaction?

- ☐ What specific factors contributed to this balance between curiosity and focus?

- ☐ If you could replicate this alignment in other areas of your work, what practices might you carry forward?

Reflect on a moment when curiosity felt overwhelming within your team or organization:

- ☐ How did the influx of ideas affect your ability to prioritize tasks and complete projects?

- What were the consequences of not having a clear focus amidst so much curiosity?

- How could clearer boundaries around curiosity and ideation have created a more productive outcome?

Consider an experience where a lack of curiosity impacted your workplace culture:

- What did this environment look and feel like, and how did it affect your motivation?

- What opportunities for innovation or improvement might have been missed due to this low curiosity?

- If you could revisit that experience, what questions would you ask to open up new possibilities?

Think about your own curiosity setpoint in relation to your current role:

- Does your natural curiosity level align well with your organization's culture?

- What impact does this have on your engagement and likelihood of staying?

- How might you adjust your approach to curiosity to find a better balance?

Reflect on a time when a leader's curiosity created distraction rather than direction:

- ☐ How did this leader's approach to curiosity impact team productivity and morale?

- ☐ What could they have done differently to maintain a focused, goal-oriented environment?

- ☐ If you are in a leadership role, how can you ensure your curiosity supports rather than overwhelms your team?

Consider how you might foster a curiosity setpoint within your team or organization:

- ☐ What steps could you take to encourage curiosity while providing clear priorities?

- ☐ How might you create a culture where curiosity is valued but balanced with actionable focus?

- ☐ What practices could help you channel curiosity in ways that lead to meaningful progress?

Curiosity Is Good Business – Key Insights

- ☐ Employee disengagement poses a significant and growing economic challenge.

- ☐ Organizations that cultivate curiosity gain advantages in employee satisfaction, innovation, and financial performance.

- ☐ The Lab 201 study identified a strong correlation between workplace curiosity and positive business outcomes.

- ☐ Many workplaces still undervalue curiosity, contributing to "quiet quitting" and loss of creative potential.

- ☐ Leaders must create environments where curiosity is encouraged at all levels to unlock hidden potential.

Part II

THE CURIOSITY CURVE

Each chapter in this section delves deeply into one of the dimensions of the Curiosity Curve, unpacking its role, benefits, and practical applications. We begin with *exploration*, the spark of curiosity that drives us to seek out new challenges and opportunities. From there, we'll examine *focused engagement*, the discipline to channel curiosity into meaningful, goal-oriented work. Next, we explore *inspirational creativity*, the ability to imagine fresh possibilities and transform ideas into innovation. Finally, we'll look at *openness to new ideas*, the willingness to embrace diverse perspectives and implement the best ones.

As we move through these chapters, you'll find actionable insights, real-world examples, and reflection points designed to help you cultivate these dimensions in your own life and work. Whether you're an individual contributor or a leader shaping organizational culture, the Curiosity Curve offers a road map to unlocking the transformative power of curiosity. Let's get curious.

4

THE FOUR FACTORS OF CURIOUS COMPANIES

Curiosity is a matter of strategic choice. The decisions we make as leaders, team members, and visionaries don't just shape our own behavior—they create ripples that affect the culture of curiosity throughout an organization. Curiosity shapes how we adapt to change, seize new opportunities, and innovate in ways that make a lasting impact. In our research for the Curiosity Curve, we found that a company's curiosity level can be understood through four specific dimensions that reflect its cultural attitude toward curiosity. We call these the *curiosity growth factors* because of the ways they influence both individual performance and collective success.

These four factors—exploration, focused engagement, inspirational creativity, and openness to new ideas—provide a framework for understanding and measuring an organization's curiosity. Together, they create a lens through which to assess the broader culture of curiosity within a company. However, each factor impacts curiosity in a distinct way, revealing nuances in how curiosity can be harnessed and nurtured for optimal growth and achievement.

> Curiosity isn't just an individual trait—it's a team and organizational advantage.

The first two factors, exploration and focused engagement, are often driven by individual actions and affect the ways people seek out, process, and implement new information. Exploration refers to the drive to look beyond the familiar, to discover what lies beyond the conventional, and to investigate new areas that might unlock opportunities for growth and innovation. Individuals with high levels of exploration are energized by novelty and demonstrate a willingness to take calculated risks. They're the ones digging into new technologies, challenging assumptions, or identifying emerging trends that might benefit the organization in the long term.

Focused engagement, on the other hand, is about channeling curiosity into purposeful action. It's not enough to merely explore possibilities; focused engagement requires that people bring their insights back to the core mission and goals of the organization. This factor ensures that curiosity doesn't dissipate into distraction but instead becomes a catalyst for problem-solving, enhanced productivity, and strategic advancement. Leaders who cultivate focused engagement set clear priorities and help their teams apply their curiosity where it will have the greatest impact.

The remaining two factors—inspirational creativity and openness to new ideas—operate on a broader, more collective level. These elements shape the organization's cultural backbone and influence the ways teams collaborate, share insights, and spark innovation together. Inspirational creativity is about fostering an environment where imaginative thinking is encouraged and where creative problem-solving is not only accepted but celebrated. Organizations that embrace this factor give their people the space to experiment, ideate, and connect the dots in novel ways. Inspirational creativity is often driven by leaders who encourage unconventional approaches, which can energize teams and bring diverse perspectives to the table.

Openness to new ideas is the final, vital component of a culture of curiosity. It reflects an organization's collective willingness to receive, consider, and integrate new perspectives. When an organization prioritizes openness, it signals to employees that their voices and ideas matter, and it nurtures an environment where everyone feels empowered to contribute. This factor is especially important for fostering inclusivity, as it allows organizations to embrace a range of viewpoints and adapt swiftly to shifting markets, technologies, and customer expectations.

Throughout this chapter, I introduce these four curiosity growth factors to help you reflect on your organization's culture of curiosity. Each factor provides insights into the overall climate, giving you a blueprint for understanding where your organization stands and where there's room to grow. I also touch on the important role of leadership in setting the tone for curiosity, with particular insight into the unique contributions women bring to this dynamic. In many organizations, women have been instrumental in cultivating cultures that value curiosity, fostering high-performing teams by encouraging diverse ideas, balanced exploration, and collaborative problem-solving.

Curiosity-driven leadership isn't just about generating new ideas; it's about knowing how to harness them, focusing energy in ways that deliver real, lasting impact. With the foundation of these four factors, you'll be equipped to delve deeper into each one in the chapters that follow, where I explore actionable strategies for leaders, managers, and teams, providing specific tools and insights to strengthen the role of curiosity within your organization. By the end, you'll have a clear understanding of how to cultivate a balanced, strategically curious culture that drives sustainable growth and innovation.

CURIOSITY = GROWTH

There are many aspects that determine the success of an organization, but our research shows that exploration, focused engagement, inspirational creativity, and openness to new ideas are key aspects of curiosity that lead to growth.

> The Curiosity Curve is a proven framework for unlocking higher performance and innovation.

Exploration refers to the ability to seek out new experiences, ideas, and challenges to expand knowledge and foster adaptability.

Focused engagement is the capacity to immerse yourself in tasks, problem-solving, and innovation with undivided attention.

Inspirational creativity is tuning in to imagination, resourcefulness, and innovative thinking as inspiration when faced with challenges.

Openness to new ideas means the willingness to embrace new information, concepts, and perspectives without immediate judgment, prejudice, or jumping to conclusions.

My fellow researchers and I were surprised when we plotted each of the four factors against our measures of success—job satisfaction, employee engagement, and job tenure. We wondered whether any of the factors would be the most significant leverage point: the place to intervene first.

Instead, we found that all four growth factors are valuable points of change. In Figure 4.1, each y axis represents employee engagement, while each x axis represents one of the four growth factors. As you can see, when exploration rises, employee engagement goes up. The same is true for focused engagement, inspirational creativity, and openness to new ideas. We found similar consistency in job satisfaction and tenure.

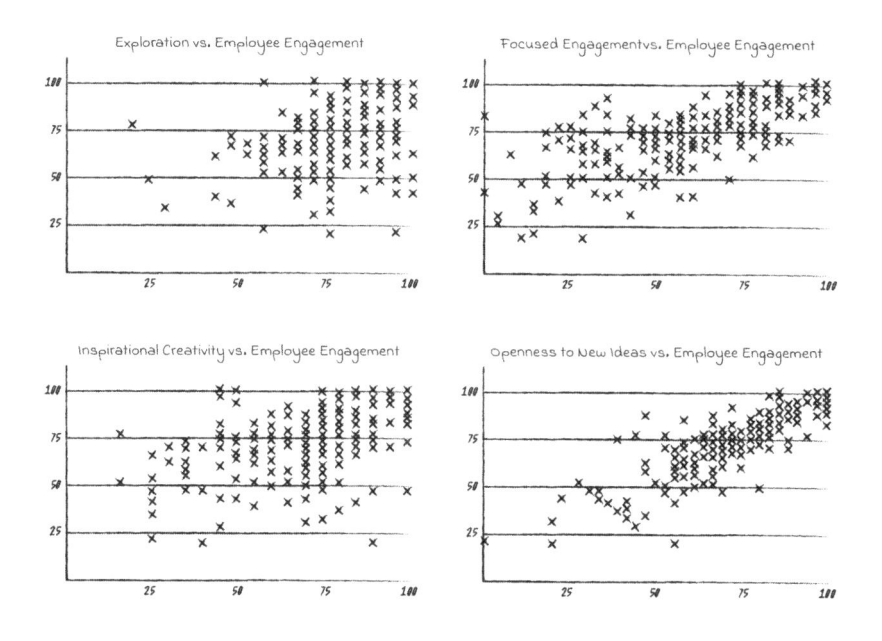

Figure 4.1: Four growth factors vs. employee engagement

Source: Lab 201, Curiosity Curve survey, 2023

THE CURIOUS LEADER

Show me a curious leader, and I'll show you a curious company culture. Culture and leadership are synonymous.

Most leaders are aware of the importance of curiosity. When I give talks about curiosity, they are usually interested. Like the CEO of Humana, who first sparked my interest in this subject, they recognize the curiosity gap in their companies. They have spent enough time struggling with people who could be raising ideas but don't. They are surrounded by people who ask questions they already know the answers to or who rarely express interest in something around them except when prodded to do so.

Leaders in companies wait for others to express curiosity while everyone else waits for them to do the same.

When a leader is curious, the definition of leadership changes. It is no longer the exercise of authority or the setting of direction. It means giving people a chance to be heard, seen, and valued.

My first question when learning about a new company is: How curious is the leader?

People have different ways of assessing this. Leaders of companies are continually being observed, so there is a great deal of data to interpret. At the same time, it is often highly stylized. You may not get a good read on a CEO's curiosity level from the jokes they tell or the words they use (as I note about curious people in Chapter 1).

Here's where the four factors come into play:

1. **Exploration:** When new opportunities or challenges are raised that seem promising, does the CEO pay attention? Is there a potential budget allocated to learning about the implications? Does the CEO express interest in the results of that initial exploration?

2. **Focused engagement:** Does the CEO lose interest in projects before they are completed? Are there clear priorities set for the company, with curiosity channeled down those paths? Does the CEO build strong working relationships with key people throughout the enterprise, particularly in the innovation and production domains?

3. **Inspirational creativity:** Does the CEO take pleasure in product launches and new offerings? Is it easy to raise questions and collaborate at the top levels of the company? Do people recognize the CEO's priorities and feel interested in taking part?

4. **Openness to new ideas:** Does the CEO express interest in concepts from outside the strict domains of the company? Are there diverse teams, with people who have different backgrounds and ways of thinking, at the top of the organizational hierarchy? Is there always a sense that the CEO will pull an amazing new offering or idea seemingly out of thin air?

In short, does the boss show evidence of curiosity? And is it optimal curiosity—open-ended enough to explore unexpected directions, yet focused enough to deliver results? It's crucial to note, though, that curiosity is not solely the domain of the CEO or top executives. While it's essential that those at the highest levels lead with curiosity, setting the tone for the organization, the impact of curiosity extends to leaders at every level.

A curious culture thrives when curiosity flows up, down, and across an organization. Show me a curious leader, and I'll show you a curious culture.

Managers, team leads, and even frontline supervisors play pivotal roles in fostering an environment where curiosity can flourish. These leaders often have a direct influence on their teams' daily experiences, guiding how curiosity is applied to specific projects, customer interactions, and problem-solving initiatives. When leaders at all levels ask questions, encourage exploration, and remain open to new ideas, they actively create the conditions for innovative thinking and continuous learning.

The good news is that just as curiosity can be cultivated as a personal skill, it can also be developed as a leadership approach. Anyone in a position of influence—whether leading a small team or a major division—can grow their ability to lead with curiosity. By nurturing a mindset that values exploration and learning, leaders at all levels can contribute to a culture of curiosity that ultimately benefits the entire organization.

LEARNING TO BE A CURIOUS LEADER

Optimal curiosity is a powerful objective. It embodies balance. You are always at the edge of novelty, with just enough novelty to stay interested but not so much that you are stretched or exhausted.

A leader in an organization embodies this. It becomes a frame of mind. There is a continual level of self-monitoring to keep the momentum going.

If the boss is sufficiently curious, so are the employees. People tend to match the curiosity level of their leaders. The study I completed found that the longer someone has been in a job, the more likely it is that they'll match the curiosity level of the company's culture. This is certainly true of most successful leaders.

The CEOs themselves may not always be aware of how much curiosity they project. Not long ago, I coached 14 members of an executive team: the CEO and his direct reports. We measured everyone's curiosity score based on their responses to our survey. When we aggregated the scores of the direct reports of the team, including the CEO, we found they scored extremely high in openness to new ideas, except for one individual. These were people who consistently sought inspiration and opportunities from a range of sources. Many of them were seasoned world travelers who had ventured into unfamiliar environments, explored new cultures, and engaged in diverse experiences. This global perspective wasn't just a background detail; it directly influenced their approach to leadership. They approached challenges with fresh perspectives, frequently drawing on cross-cultural insights and innovative practices they had encountered abroad.

Their openness to new ideas was reflected in how they brought outside inspiration back to the organization, constantly looking for ways to push boundaries and adapt to change. This experience underscored an essential insight: While the CEO's curiosity sets a powerful example, it's the curiosity of those at every level—often shaped by their unique experiences and worldviews—that drives a culture of curiosity throughout the company.

And yet, the company itself had a relatively poor track record in innovation. They launched many new products, but these products often faltered.

The one individual that had the low score on openness to new ideas was the CEO. He said, "That low score is me, and I think I might be shutting people down without realizing it."

"How do you feel about that?" I asked the team. "Does that seem like a reasonable perception?" (We had built up enough psychological safety to have this conversation as a group.)

They agreed it was. "He doesn't listen to our ideas," someone said. Apparently, he listened even less to people outside the executive team. Later, when I coached him one-on-one, he explained how he felt: "I kind of feel like I have all the good ideas, and I know what to do." His long-standing experience as a founder at the helm of the company had convinced him of this.

This is one reason why organizational change work often involves individual and group coaching. Leaders will typically find it easier to realize the truth about their curiosity when they are together with their executive teams. But to think about what they've learned and how they might want to change their behavior or pay attention differently, they need a chance to reflect and adjust.

In the team retreat, people can see aggregate scores and get a better sense of where they agree and where they don't. They can figure out the sources of friction on the team versus the sources of constructive disagreements. They can suggest changes and pose questions such as, "If we want to be a high-performance team, what are some of the things that we need to stop doing? What should we start doing or continue doing?"

Since that session, the goals of the leadership team for this particular organization have shifted. They now pay attention to the number of projects underway at their level. No longer are there any pet projects hidden from the group. At their monthly meetings, they go through the list. Projects that are no longer useful are discontinued. New projects are introduced. If there are fewer than 10 major projects company-wide, the team senses that the CEO is shutting down ideas again. If there are more than 20 on the list, they recognize that they have lost their focus and need to converge. This rough estimate has become their rule of thumb.

The CEO is still the arbiter of projects and a significant source of judgment. But he no longer believes that his is the only opinion that matters. As it turns out, many projects that he would have shut down have become profitable after he let them proceed. His role now is far more collaborative than it had been. He has become a living embodiment of the curiosity of the company, inspiring others and laying the groundwork for the company's success after he retires. He is curious to see what it could do then.

How does a leader learn to do this—to inspire curiosity in others? How does an executive learn to give people a chance to be heard, seen, and valued?

There are several behavioral practices that can make all the difference. You don't have to wait to be a CEO; they can be practiced at any level of leadership in an organization, whether you're in the C-suite or a first-time team lead on a project.

Ask Open-Ended Questions

One way to build your curiosity capabilities is to ask open-ended questions, where you are sincerely curious about the answer and authentically want to learn. You have to recognize that others may see things you do not, and you have to demonstrate a reasonably high level of compassion and kindness. You may have to put your ego on the table, showing a willingness to learn rather than prove a point. And this often means being dispassionate about your current perspective, especially if the answers challenge or even contradict it.

Not all questions are created equal, however. It's important to distinguish between genuine and nongenuine questions.

Genuine questions are those that open the way for a wide variety of answers. These questions invite the other person to share their unique perspective without fearing judgment, creating space for insights and ideas you may not have considered.

For instance, instead of asking, "Don't you think this project could be improved by doing X?"—which subtly guides the answer—a genuine question might be, "What do you see as the biggest opportunity to improve this project?"

This type of question reflects true openness and sets aside any attachment to a particular answer, allowing for fresh input. Genuine questions are rooted in a desire to understand, to learn something new, and to view the situation from someone else's vantage point. By asking these questions, you signal a willingness to engage in collaborative exploration, where the outcome isn't predetermined.

Nongenuine questions, on the other hand, are those that subtly or overtly lead the respondent toward a specific answer. Often posed with an underlying agenda, these questions suggest that the person asking is seeking confirmation rather than information. For example, "Don't you think this is the best solution?" implies that the asker is looking for agreement rather than feedback. While such questions may appear to open up a dialogue, they actually close down the opportunity for others to contribute freely. As a result, they limit curiosity, creativity, and growth by steering the conversation back to the asker's preconceived views.

The difference between genuine and nongenuine questions can profoundly shape conversations, leading to either new insights or missed opportunities. By prioritizing genuine questions, you cultivate a culture of curiosity that values diverse perspectives and fuels collective learning.

Genuine versus Nongenuine Questions

Genuine questions (spark exploration and openness): Genuine questions encourage exploration, deepen understanding, and show a willingness to listen and learn. They open the door to possibility and collaboration. For example:

- ☐ What are we missing here that could change the way we see this problem?

- ☐ How did you arrive at this idea, and what inspired it?

- ☐ What are the biggest opportunities or risks you see in this situation?

- ☐ If we could take all constraints off the table, what might we try instead?

- ☐ How does your experience shape the way you're approaching this?

- ☐ What's the most unexpected thing you've learned while exploring this?

- ☐ If you were in the shoes of someone affected by this, how might you feel or respond?

- ☐ What's the smallest step we could take to test or refine this idea?

- ☐ How might this align with or challenge our long-term goals?

- ☐ What's one question we haven't asked yet that might help us move forward?

Nongenuine questions (shut down possibilities): Nongenuine questions often come with hidden judgments or assumptions. They can stifle creativity, put others on the defensive, and shut down meaningful dialogue:

- ☐ Why don't you understand why this won't work?

- ☐ Who thought that was a good idea?

- ☐ Don't you realize how much time we've wasted on this already?

- ☐ Why didn't you just stick with the original plan?

- ☐ Can't we all just agree this is a bad idea?

- ☐ What made you think you could handle this without consulting the team?

- ☐ Aren't you overcomplicating things unnecessarily?

- ☐ Why can't we just do what's worked before?

- ☐ Isn't this just another way of saying your idea didn't pan out?

- ☐ What's wrong with you that you didn't think of this sooner?

The difference between genuine and nongenuine questions lies in intent and openness. Genuine questions come from a place of curiosity and respect, seeking to learn or uncover new possibilities. Nongenuine questions, by contrast, often mask criticism, assumptions, or impatience, shutting down creativity and collaboration.

By choosing our questions carefully, we create environments where curiosity can flourish, trust can grow, and solutions can emerge that no one person could have arrived at alone. A genuine question, asked at the right time, has the power to shift perspectives, unlock innovation, and deepen relationships.

Practice Active Listening

This simple act can lay the groundwork for a culture of curiosity and help employees feel valued. It can also enhance problem-solving, decision-making, and conflict-resolution skills. It tends to produce a more comprehensive understanding of the issues at hand.

Active listening requires the willingness to be silent and concentrate on what someone else is saying. It goes beyond simply hearing the words. The listener should be fully present, paying attention to the speech but also to nonverbal cues like nodding. Don't interrupt or think about what you're going to say next.

This type of listening demonstrates genuine curiosity—along with respect, empathy, and a genuine interest in understanding their perspectives. If you don't feel those attributes, the practice of active listening can help put you in the frame of mind to adopt them. If you are bored, the experience of active listening may paradoxically make it easier to change the subject because the speaker knows you have been paying full attention.

To practice active listening, focus on maintaining eye contact and thinking about the words. When the speaker is finished, you can follow up by asking clarifying questions or paraphrasing what was said to demonstrate you understood. You can also frame the whole conversation at the end by summing up what was discussed or asking, "What are we going to do about this?" By consistently employing these techniques, leaders can foster a culture of open communication, trust, and collaboration within their organizations.

Embrace Feedback

A positive relationship to feedback—responses from others about your attitudes or behavior—is a clear indicator of genuine curiosity. The ability to receive feedback without defensiveness is also a hallmark of effective leadership. A person's relationship to feedback is one of the strongest predictors of their career trajectory. Curious leaders actively seek feedback because they understand it's a powerful tool for uncovering things they were not conscious of, identifying areas for improvement, and building trust with their teams. They view feedback not as criticism but as a valuable perspective that helps them grow and adapt. This openness allows them to better understand how they're perceived, how their actions impact others, and where they might need to adjust their approach to lead more effectively.

Receiving feedback well takes practice, and a strong foundation for it is a commitment to your own growth—an openness to expanding your knowledge and an intent to communicate effectively with your team or organization. This mindset not only strengthens individual development but fosters a collaborative, high-trust environment where curiosity and improvement are welcomed at all levels.

Questions for Feedback

Seeking feedback requires humility, openness, and a willingness to grow. These questions are designed to invite honest and constructive input while fostering trust and collaboration:

- ☐ *Have I said or done anything that may have contributed to this issue, even unintentionally?* This question shows accountability and signals that you are open to self-reflection, making it easier for others to share their perspectives.

- ☐ *Is there something I might not be seeing or fully understanding in this situation?* Acknowledging weaknesses demonstrates curiosity and a desire to understand the issue more deeply from multiple angles.

- ☐ *What would be the most helpful way for me to support you or the team right now?* This question positions you as a collaborative partner and shifts the focus toward actionable solutions.

By asking these types of questions, you not only gain valuable insights but also strengthen relationships and create a culture of openness and mutual respect.

Form and Test Hypotheses

In an organization without much regard for curiosity, we experience problems as tension. They are issues that must be resolved quickly so that we can feel relief.

The employee places a problem on the table. No one expects the employee to solve it; otherwise, it would have already been taken care of. The leader is expected to know the answer. If we're the leader, we look for the answer that's at the top of our minds. We then provide the solution to the employee. Curiosity is not in the equation at all.

In a curious company, the employee raises a problem that deserves more consideration. It may be raised to a team doing the work or escalated to a more senior leader. Either way, people assume there's something going on here worth exploring. They are curious about it. If they can handle it, they can probably handle other things as well.

They might start by asking questions such as, "What do we know about this?" The leader may ask the employee to step back and recount how the problem came to their attention and why it seems to matter.

Instead of jumping to a solution, the group comes up with a hypothesis. This problem occurred because something is causing something else.

Then, they test the hypothesis. They perform the action at a small scale. If it works, they might scale it up or adjust it. If it doesn't work, then they invoke their curiosity again, letting it guide them to another hypothesis.

The leader's curiosity is active throughout the case. The leader asks, suggests, proposes, listens, and gets involved in the test. People interact together as peers. It feels powerful to work this way: our curiosity is the tide, and we ride it into shore.

Unlearning

In Chapter 1, I proposed that we learn to become incurious throughout our lives. This serves us well in childhood, where curiosity may annoy others. It allows us to rise in school, in college, and in our workplaces. We become especially incurious if we become experts relied on for our specialized insight and knowledge. At that point, to admit curiosity might feel like betraying our profession.

But then we become leaders. We are responsible for great enterprises with many diverse people and systems. If we're not curious, we won't succeed.

So we have to learn to unlearn. We have to abandon those habits we've picked up since childhood and go backward. From asking only 5 questions a day as adults, we have to regain our ability to ask 396, as we did when we were toddlers.

Self-curiosity begins with unlearning. As business leader and futurist Alvin Toffler wrote in his book *Future Shock*: "By instructing students how to learn, unlearn and relearn, a powerful new dimension can be added to education."[1] In that context, he added that "Tomorrow's illiterate will not be the [person] who can't read, but the person who has not learned how to learn"—with unlearning as part of the equation. Toffler himself was regarded, throughout his life, as an example of this approach, continually driven by his own curiosity.

Business theorist Chris Argyris framed unlearning as a three-part, never-ending cycle. We learn values, beliefs, vision, and awareness. We unlearn limited beliefs, limiting perceptions, and things that no longer serve us. We then relearn new ways, reframe our perspective, and absorb new skills and a new mindset.[2]

Even if you haven't read these two theorists, you've probably heard of decluttering: the concept popularized by Marie Kondo and others, in which you remove elements from your physical environment that bring you no joy.[3] Unlearning is a similar process for the mind. You remove beliefs and attitudes that no longer serve you, if they ever did. As executive coach Marshall Goldsmith puts it, "What got you here will not get you there."[4]

There's a discipline to it. It requires you to be curious about yourself and your thoughts. You may need to challenge your beliefs in a loving way, embracing them so they can no longer disturb you. You may ask yourself: Why do I believe what I believe? The answer is that somebody taught you: your parents, your schools, your workplace, or some other part of yourself. There may be roots in elemental hatred, anger, grief, or violence that no longer has real meaning but that somehow keeps popping up in your thoughts.

One way to begin the practice of unlearning is with reflective meditation, which can help you break down the origins of your thoughts, attitudes, behaviors, feelings, and biases. You can practice this right now. Put yourself in a relatively peaceful frame of mind, in a comfortable place, with half an hour to dedicate to the following exercise.

Meditation for Unlearning

Unlearning begins with curiosity and reflection. This meditation is designed to help you challenge and release beliefs that may no longer serve you, creating space for growth and transformation.

Identify a Belief to Challenge

Choose one belief you hold about your company, your work, or your life that you feel may be limiting your potential. Write it down clearly and honestly. Let yourself sit with it, fully experiencing what it feels like to hold this belief. Read it aloud, allowing its weight and meaning to resonate.

Reflect and Question the Belief

Use these prompts to gently examine the belief:

- ☐ **Where did this belief originate?**
  Explore its roots. Was it shaped by personal experiences, societal norms, or the influence of others?

- ☐ **Is this belief objectively true?**
  Look for evidence that supports or challenges its validity.

- ☐ **How do I know it's true?**
  Consider whether your perception is based on facts or assumptions.

Assess the Belief's Impact

Ask yourself these deeper questions to uncover how this belief affects you:

- ☐ **Does this belief support my mental and emotional well-being?**
  Evaluate whether it uplifts you or weighs you down.

- ☐ **Is this belief aligned with the life I want to create?**
  Consider whether it helps you move closer to your goals and aspirations.

- ☐ **Is this belief congruent with the person I aspire to become?**
  Reflect on whether it fosters growth, authenticity, and integrity.

> ☐ **Is this belief true to who I am at my core?**
> Examine if it resonates with your deepest values and identity.
>
> **Reframe or Release**
> If the belief no longer serves you, write a new belief to replace it—one that is more empowering, truthful, and aligned with your vision for the future. Let yourself feel the freedom of this new perspective.

Unlearning isn't about discarding everything you've known—it's about making intentional choices to let go of what limits you and embrace beliefs that expand your possibilities. This practice encourages clarity, courage, and curiosity, leading you closer to the life and career you truly want.

Unlearning is a process that never ends. Just as we embrace life-long learning, we need lifelong unlearning. The ability to do this is like a superpower: It sparks creativity, allows you to see new and different perspectives, and improves relationships.

Most of all, it retunes your curiosity. Unlearning prepares us for the future.

CURIOUS LEADERSHIP AND WOMEN

Our research on curiosity in the workplace allowed us to collect and analyze gender data as well. We wanted to see if either men or women were more likely to report themselves as curious.

We were somewhat surprised by the results: There was no significant difference, at least not in our study, between male and female respondents. The same was true for the other studies we looked at. Sometimes men expressed more curiosity, and sometimes women did, but the variation was always less than 2 percentage points.

But another finding suggested a more significant difference. A group of researchers based in Europe and the US observed 250 departmental seminars in 35 academic institutions, where professors and graduate students exchange new findings in science and social science. They found that women were 2.5 times less likely to ask a question than men. This reluctance was especially notable when a man asked the first question after a talk, setting a tone that seemed to discourage women from participating.[5]

In an accompanying survey of 600 students, women acknowledged this reluctance and gave several reasons: they didn't feel clever enough, they couldn't work up the nerve, they worried about their understanding, or they felt intimidated by the speaker's expertise or reputation. Men, in contrast, reported few, if any, of these curiosity-killing inhibitions.[6]

In the workplace, this trend often appears as hesitation to take bold steps or assert oneself fully in discussions and decision-making. I've observed women in leadership meetings who hold back when proposing ideas or sharing insights, fearing they may be perceived as overly assertive or insufficiently prepared. Some have shared with me that they hesitate to take risks in pitching ideas, believing they must be exceptionally well-polished to avoid scrutiny. Others avoid asking probing questions in meetings led by senior male colleagues, concerned that their curiosity may be misinterpreted as overstepping boundaries. For women, especially those in male-dominated fields, curiosity can feel like a double-edged sword; they know it can signal initiative and engagement, but they're equally aware that it might expose them to judgment.

This reality could be tied to the ways women's lives and experiences differ from men's from an early age. Could it be that from childhood, all the factors that make people less inclined to be curious affect women more deeply than men? Perhaps women are subtly, or sometimes overtly, discouraged from the perceived risks of curiosity—especially in high-stakes professional settings where questions or new ideas may invite criticism.

The realities of women's lives can indeed make curiosity a complex balancing act. Too much curiosity, and they risk standing out in ways that may lead to criticism or alienation. Too little, and they risk missing out on growth, visibility, and the opportunity to challenge the status quo. For women, cultivating curiosity in the workplace often means navigating a fine line, one that is less about interest alone and more about gauging the right moment, the right approach, and the likely response from those around them.

Letting Women Speak

In a conversation with Julie Castro Abrams, managing partner of How Women Invest and CEO of How Women Lead. These organizations promote venture fund investment in women-run entrepreneurial businesses and support for women's executive roles. She is a leading expert on the process of placing women on corporate boards, where their influence often favors more compassionate, service-oriented, environmentally aware practices—and more curiosity in general. She is also a philanthropist who founded an organization called How Women Give. Many of these successes came out of a lifelong drive to follow her curiosity.[7]

During her 12-year tenure as the founder and first CEO of the Women's Initiative for Self Employment, a San Francisco-based nonprofit providing guidance and lending support to low-income women entrepreneurs, Julie witnessed firsthand the systemic challenges women faced in accessing capital. When the financial crisis unfolded in 2010, she became increasingly intrigued by the broader lack of opportunities for women entrepreneurs. At the time, out of all the startups in Silicon Valley and beyond funded by venture capital, only about a dozen had been founded by women without a male partner.

"There was no pathway for women to get funding," she said. "It was a very bad scene."

It's easy to jump to conclusions about why. Maybe there was a shortage of qualified women entrepreneurs—except that Julie knew many capable women entrepreneurs from her years at the Women's Initiative. Maybe men had closed women out—but again, there was a large group of wealthy female investors emerging. Or maybe the reason was related to the shortage of women in venture capital. Most likely it was a complex system involving a shortage of women on boards and in venture funds, a lack of laws mandating women's presence in those realms, entrenched investment habits, endemic sexism and racism in the field, and the sheer time it takes to change all these factors, especially in a stodgy field like finance.

Sometimes, the best way to understand a complex system is to poke your nose in and see what will happen. In that spirit, Julie began following her curiosity down several paths.

One of those paths involved promoting diversity on the boards of publicly held companies. Influenced by advocacy efforts, including Julie's, California passed laws requiring companies to reserve seats for women and underrepresented communities. The laws were in place from 2018 to 2022, when they were targeted by lawsuits and declared unconstitutional (the gender law is still under appeal). Meanwhile, the presence of women on those boards moved from 23% to 32% within five years.[8]

In 2018, California enacted Senate Bill 826 (SB 826), mandating that publicly traded companies headquartered in the state include a specified number of women on their boards of directors. The law required these companies to have at least one female director by the end of 2019, with the number increasing based on board size by the end of 2021. Following the implementation of SB 826, the representation of women on corporate boards in California saw a significant increase. Women held 15.5% of board seats in 2018, which rose to 31.9% by the end of 2021.[9]

However, in May 2022, a Los Angeles Superior Court judge ruled that SB 826 violated the Equal Protection Clause of the California Constitution, rendering the law unconstitutional.[10]

Despite this legal setback, the proportion of women on corporate boards in California had already increased significantly during the law's enforcement period. The increase in women's representation on corporate boards has been documented over the years in several reports.

Here are some notable sources and dates:

1. **Harvard Law School's "Women in the Boardroom" Report (2022):** This report noted that as of 2022, women held 19.7% of board seats globally, reflecting a steady increase. This was up by 2.8 percentage points from 2019, showing continued progress in gender diversity on boards worldwide.[11]

2. **Fortune 500 Board Data (2023):** In the United States, women held over 30% of board seats on Fortune 500 companies in 2022, up from 26.5% in 2020. This report

by Deloitte highlighted the pace of change in US corporate leadership diversity.[12]

These reports show a significant increase in gender representation on corporate boards within the past decade, illustrating the global efforts to achieve gender parity in leadership.

Clearly, legal oversight was not the only path to follow. Based near Silicon Valley, Julie was well aware of the pay inequity at most tech companies. As she told me, "They try to do audits and adjust it, but it's always broken. That's because we don't have good, balanced leadership."

She therefore began looking at private equity. It turned out that less than 2% of all venture fund capital went to companies founded by women. That might mean just $3 billion out of a total $170 billion in a year. "That's egregious," Julie says. "It doesn't make any sense. I'll give the market a pass saying until today, there maybe weren't enough women experienced in the startup world. But there's no excuse going forward. The number of experienced female entrepreneurs is now huge. We have power, influence, wealth, and operational expertise galore. And there's no way you can change who's on private boards unless you start with the investors."

In 2020, Julie launched How Women Invest as a funder's platform and seed fund for women investing in women. It is the only VC fund in the US that exclusively finances companies founded by women with no male cofounders. So far, they've raised three rounds: the first two of $10 million each, and the third of $100 million. A five-year goal is to have $1 billion in assets under management, all invested in female-run companies.[13]

On the investor side, the fund has started a New Table Campaign, attracting smaller amounts from women investors. Their goal is to attract 10,000 women to invest in venture funds for the first time, with more than 50 women-run entrepreneurial firms to choose from. "There's a platform you can use to research and meet them," Julie explained. "There might be one aligned with your values. Check it out. Take the class, learn, read the material." So far, they've signed up 1,400 small investors, many with $100,000 or more of capital. As the numbers accumulate, the fund is developing clout. "Women have 52% of the wealth," says Julie, "and only 5% of the women who *can* invest in venture, actually invest in venture. To me, here's an opportunity to change that."

This type of network-based investing also introduces more women to the status and clout that comes with the venture arena. "When you say you're an investor in venture funds, people think of you differently. Somehow you now have some knowledge, access, courage, or something. It paints you in a different way. I want more women making the money you can make in venture capital, but I also want us to be in the game—to get that power and aura." It's also meaningful work. By becoming a VC investor, women can influence the people who are on the board, which also influences the direction of the company.

Meanwhile, Julie also launched a discussion series called "How Women Lead." It started in 2019 with just 100 participants, all in San Francisco.

Again, curiosity took the lead. "I started How Women Lead because I wanted to hang out with great women, with no real intention except letting me keep up these beautiful relationships with people I hadn't seen for a bit," Julie said. "So I held a series of small meetups in San Francisco, and from the first day, I saw everyone was so excited to be together. People kept talking to each other, even when the speaker was onstage. No one wanted to leave. They were all entrepreneurs, and they hadn't really ever met women leaders."

The group began as an informal gathering at a bar but evolved during the pandemic into a weekly Zoom meeting with 6,000 women invited (although not all attended each time). What started as casual social gatherings grew into larger fundraising breakfasts with 400 to 800 participants. When the pandemic hit, it transformed into a platform where women leaders could connect regularly, meeting weekly at first and then flexing the schedule as people settled into new routines. By the time in-person events resumed, the group had become a more formal organization, offering courses and structured programming. Today, over 22,000 women have participated in at least one event, with nearly 200,000 following the group on LinkedIn. Events now take place in cities across the US and in Mexico, creating a widespread community of women leaders.

The point of this story is to illustrate the power of curiosity in action—especially when that curiosity is our own. Even though our Curiosity Curve research found no statistically significant differences between men's and women's curiosity levels, I continue to have a hunch. There is something real and significant here that isn't captured entirely by the data but resonates deeply with experience.

Curiosity isn't just essential for women as individuals who want to grow and lead effectively—it's essential for organizations to recognize the transformative value that curious women leaders bring to the table. Women who ask questions, challenge norms, and explore new possibilities foster environments that encourage innovation, resilience, and inclusivity. They bring unique insights and often bridge perspectives across teams, enriching organizational culture and decision-making.

Organizations that actively support and promote women in leadership roles tap into a well of curiosity that enhances adaptability and drives sustainable success.

The larger point here is that curiosity, when cultivated and valued in women leaders, amplifies the overall potential of a business. Women's curiosity doesn't just benefit individual careers; it strengthens organizations by introducing fresh perspectives and adaptive strategies, creating ripple effects that improve team performance, employee engagement, and innovation. For companies looking to stay competitive, promoting and nurturing curiosity in women isn't just a good practice—it's a strategic advantage.

❋

In this chapter, we've introduced the four factors of curiosity—exploration, focused engagement, inspirational creativity, and openness to new ideas—and discussed some ways in which curious leaders can position themselves to be receptive to curiosity. We'll now examine all four factors in greater detail.

> ### Curiosity Reflection
> **Reflect on a time when your curiosity led you to join or build a community:**
>
> - ☐ How did your curiosity shape the connections you made or the insights you gained?
>
> - ☐ What impact did this community have on your personal or professional growth?

- ☐ How might you continue fostering curiosity within this community to keep it dynamic and engaging?

Think about how you approach curiosity in your leadership role or workplace:

- ☐ Do you actively seek out perspectives that challenge your assumptions? If so, how?

- ☐ What steps can you take to encourage curiosity-driven conversations within your team?

- ☐ How could promoting curiosity among your team lead to greater innovation and productivity?

Consider the role of curiosity in breaking down traditional barriers in your industry:

- ☐ Where might curiosity help you or your organization explore new approaches or challenge outdated norms?

- ☐ Are there areas where a lack of curiosity could be limiting your team's potential?

- ☐ How can you lead by example in fostering a culture that values exploration and learning?

Reflect on the potential value of curious women in leadership roles within your organization:

- ☐ What specific qualities do you think women's curiosity brings to the leadership table?

- ☐ How does supporting curiosity in women leaders contribute to a more inclusive and adaptive workplace?

- ☐ What practices could you implement to ensure that curiosity is nurtured in all leaders, regardless of gender?

Think about a moment when curiosity felt like a risk:

- ☐ What were you afraid of—judgment, misunderstanding, failure?

- ☐ How did you decide whether to pursue that curiosity or hold back? What was the outcome?

- ☐ In future situations, how might you balance the risks and rewards of being openly curious?

Reflect on the importance of community for sustaining curiosity:

- ☐ How has being part of a curious community or network influenced your professional outlook?

- ☐ In what ways does a community of curious individuals help you see new possibilities or approaches?

- ☐ What actions can you take to strengthen your network, fostering curiosity as a shared value?

5
EXPLORATION

Exploration—the ability to actively seek out new ideas and challenges—is essential for personal growth, and it's imperative for organizations that want to succeed. This chapter examines the personal, team leadership, and organizational benefits of exploration and offers ideas for fostering it within your own organization.

Tracy Rector, executive producer of the 2019 film *No Ordinary Love*, became a filmmaker through exploration. A survivor of an abusive marriage, she served as chairman of the board of SafeHaven, the second-largest domestic violence agency in Texas. While reviewing a recurring report called a fatality review, which tracks the history of women killed in domestic violence cases, she realized that most of the victims had never sought shelter, counseling, or legal help. They had never called a hotline. If they had, SafeHaven's counselors could have conducted danger assessments and informed them about their risks.

"We're not getting to the women who need it most," Tracy thought. Then her curiosity kicked in: "Why is this?"

One reason was a clear lack of awareness. Many women simply didn't know about available resources. Although Tracy had majored in advertising and PR in college, she had never practiced it as a career. Now, she wondered about starting a campaign. What would it take? She considered posting signs on buses, but she was concerned that women in dire straits might not see them.

"I needed something bigger, and I just kept going to a different place in my mind. The path always led me to decide that I needed to make a movie," she said. "You can reach a huge audience that way, I told myself. It couldn't be a domestic violence documentary, because people wouldn't go watch that. It had to be a narrative. I didn't know what to do, and I kept asking myself, 'What do I do next to make this happen?'"[1]

At nearly sixty years old, and in a serious relationship, she decided to make a film for the first time in her life. She had just remodeled her house when a filmmaker named Chyna Robinson called to ask if she could use it for a short film. That led to a conversation and, from there, one stepping stone of curiosity after another. First, they needed a script and money. "You do the script," Tracy told Chyna. "I'll figure out the funding."

Tracy found investors, and they entered a pre-production phase: casting, finding sets where owners would let them film for free, and more. The initial plan was a 25-minute film. Then, an editor friend read the script and encouraged them to make it a full-length feature. Filming involved 13-hour days, followed by applications to film festivals, distribution deals, and trying to reach college audiences during the COVID-19 pandemic. Each time Tracy felt like stopping, her curiosity propelled her forward.

The film was shown at several festivals, winning awards at each, and ultimately streamed on Amazon Prime Video. "The biggest accolades were from survivors who said, 'Oh my God, I have never seen my story on the big screen like that. And I didn't realize how bad it was. I felt so validated. And it wasn't my fault. It was the abuse and the constant control and power struggle.'" Tracy shared that if she had seen a film like this at the right time, she might have left her first marriage sooner.

Serendipity played a role, certainly, but without exploration, the conversation with Chyna Robinson would have simply ended. The act of exploring keeps curiosity alive, and Tracy's story shows how personal exploration can spur professional collaboration.

This same spirit of exploration fuels innovation within established organizations, where internal structures often harness curiosity for collective growth. Consider Google's hiring process, which exemplifies exploration within a corporate environment. Rather than adhering to conventional recruitment strategies, Google takes an exploratory approach, welcoming candidates from diverse fields and even valuing nontraditional qualifications like unique life experiences. Google encourages its hiring managers to ask open-ended questions to uncover unconventional skills and insights—an approach that helps the company find candidates who bring creativity and adaptability to the table.

> Curiosity starts with exploration—the willingness to ask "what if?" and "why not?"

This exploration-driven approach extends into Google's famously flexible work environment, where employees are given "20% time" to pursue personal projects that might lead to new products or improvements. Gmail and Google News, now widely used products, originated as individual exploration projects.[2] By embracing this model, Google ensures that curiosity is not only encouraged but integral to its innovation process.

Through these examples—Tracy's creative leap and Google's structured curiosity—we see how exploration can drive impact on both personal and organizational levels. In the following section, we explore actionable ways to foster exploration within your organization, ensuring curiosity remains an essential part of your culture and fuels long-term growth and success.

HARNESSING CURIOSITY FOR EXPLORATION

In an organizational context, exploration is active. Teams and companies deliberately seek out new experiences, ideas, and challenges. They are pursuing agility, adaptability, and robust leadership, understanding that these attributes strengthen with exposure to fresh perspectives and innovative ideas.

In companies that value exploration, curiosity is woven into the cultural fabric. When challenges arise, people welcome the chance to learn and solve problems creatively. Leaders cultivate environments where employees feel free to try new approaches without fear of blame. Failures are seen as learning opportunities, and rather than micromanaging, leaders trust their teams to find their own paths to success.

Exploration also extends to potential future opportunities. Employees are encouraged to network beyond their immediate teams and collaborate on joint projects, fostering connections that spark new ideas. Their voices matter, and their development is actively supported by leaders who recognize that diverse perspectives lead to stronger solutions. By creating an environment where differences are valued, the organization builds a foundation for innovation and resilience. As a leader, you have a unique role in fostering exploration at the individual, team, and organizational levels. Your encouragement of curiosity, along with a commitment to learning and growth, can transform your organization's culture. Curious leaders set a tone of openness and innovation, inspiring others to think beyond the obvious and welcome challenges as opportunities for discovery.

At the individual level, fostering exploration means creating space for employees to pursue ideas they are passionate about, even if these ideas seem outside their usual scope. This could include supporting side projects or encouraging attendance at cross-departmental meetings or external events. When employees feel empowered to explore, they develop stronger problem-solving skills, adapt to change, and bring fresh ideas back to their roles. Encouraging personal exploration also enhances engagement; employees who feel their curiosity is valued tend to be more invested and committed to their organization.

An interesting finding in our June 2025 study of 394 professionals across industries revealed strong internal consistency in the Cultural Curiosity Scale, along with meaningful patterns.[3] Notably, "Exploration" scores increased with job level—suggesting that as individuals gain autonomy, they are more likely to seek out new approaches and challenge assumptions. This highlights a key opportunity: leaders can actively cultivate exploration by creating conditions of trust, autonomy, and psychological safety—well before people reach the C-suite.

At the team level, you can foster exploration by encouraging collaboration and cross-functional projects. Consider creating opportunities for team members to shadow colleagues in different roles or participate in "idea exchanges," where employees from various teams come together to brainstorm. Team exploration not only broadens perspectives but also strengthens trust and cohesion, as individuals feel free to share insights without fear of judgment. When leaders encourage team members to look outside their usual work boundaries, they create a dynamic environment where innovation and adaptability flourish.

At the organizational level, fostering exploration involves embedding curiosity into your company's core values. This might mean formalizing initiatives like "innovation days," where employees dedicate time to pursuing their ideas, or implementing learning stipends that allow employees to attend conferences, courses, or training sessions. Building a culture that values exploration means providing both the time and resources for employees to engage in continuous learning. You might also consider implementing "reverse mentoring" programs where employees across levels and functions can learn from one another, enriching the culture with diverse insights and experiences.

Fostering a culture of exploration is not only beneficial for individual growth, it also strengthens the organization's overall adaptability. Companies that embrace curiosity are more resilient when facing change, as they are more likely to anticipate and respond to evolving market demands. This adaptability fuels a cycle of innovation and continuous improvement, positioning your organization to lead rather than follow in its industry.

By actively promoting exploration, you lay the foundation for an organization that sees change as an opportunity, where people at all levels are empowered to bring their ideas forward, experiment, and grow. As a leader, your support of exploration can create a culture of curiosity that not only attracts talented, curious individuals but retains them, creating lasting value for your organization and building a resilient, forward-looking future.

ENCOURAGING INDIVIDUAL EXPLORATION

Dedicate time for self-directed learning
Encourage team members to set aside a few hours each month for self-directed learning and exploration. Consider providing subsidies for courses related to innovation, critical thinking, or problem-solving.

Example: Give employees "learning days" when they can focus on skill development or research a topic of interest.

Provide access to continuous learning platforms
Invest in subscriptions to learning platforms such as Coursera, LinkedIn Learning, or MasterClass to support employees' professional growth in areas like leadership, design thinking, or emerging technologies.

Example: Create a shared library of online course options, allowing team members to select what suits their interests and goals.

Encourage stretch assignments
Assign projects that push employees slightly beyond their usual scope of work. This not only encourages skill development but also inspires new ways of thinking.

Example: Offer a junior team member the chance to lead a presentation or manage a project with guidance from a mentor.

Sponsor conference and workshop attendance
Encourage employees to attend relevant conferences and workshops. Covering registration fees or travel costs demonstrates that the organization values growth.

Example: Send marketing team members to an annual industry conference, where they can gain fresh insights to share with the team.

Offer job shadowing opportunities
Allow employees to shadow colleagues in different departments to learn about diverse functions within the company. This broadens their perspective and fosters cross-functional curiosity.

Example: Let someone from marketing shadow a product developer for a day to understand the intricacies of product design.

Support mentorship and reverse mentoring
Pair employees with mentors or, in reverse mentoring, with junior colleagues who can offer fresh insights. This exchange benefits both parties, encouraging exploration from different viewpoints.

Example: A seasoned manager could be paired with a new hire proficient in the latest tech, fostering a reciprocal learning relationship.

Create a "curiosity budget"
Allocate a small annual budget for each employee to spend on personal development resources, such as books, workshops, or tools that ignite their curiosity and creativity.

Example: Give employees $100 per year to purchase books or tools that will help them explore topics they're passionate about.

Encourage knowledge-sharing sessions
After attending courses or conferences, encourage employees to share their learnings in a short presentation or

workshop for their team. This reinforces their exploration and benefits the whole team.

Example: A team member who took a storytelling course could lead a session on how to use storytelling techniques in team presentations.

Incorporate passion projects into quarterly goals
Allow employees to set quarterly goals that include a passion project related to their role or a new skill they're interested in. These projects enable exploration within a structured setting.

Example: A project manager could explore digital design, creating graphics for team presentations as a personal project.

Promote open access to industry news and research
Provide subscriptions to industry publications, journals, or newsletters, and encourage employees to stay informed about trends and innovations.

Example: Share a subscription to a publication like *Harvard Business Review* or *Fast Company,* and invite team members to circulate articles that spark ideas.

At the team level, fostering exploration is essential for creating a collaborative, innovative environment. When team members feel encouraged to be curious, share ideas freely, and learn from one another, they become more agile and adaptive in tackling challenges. As a leader, you can inspire exploration by creating opportunities for team members to cross boundaries, build connections, and experiment with new approaches together. These practices not only enhance team dynamics but also build a foundation of trust, resilience, and shared growth that strengthens the entire organization.

ENCOURAGING TEAM EXPLORATION

Practice psychological safety
Create a safe space where all team members feel comfortable sharing ideas without fear of judgment or dismissal. Psychological safety encourages open dialogue, reduces hesitancy, and helps ideas flourish.

Example: Start meetings with a reminder that "all ideas are welcome," and make it a habit to validate every contribution by acknowledging its potential.

Foster cross-departmental collaboration
Encourage team members to collaborate with colleagues in different departments. This kind of cross-boundary work broadens perspectives and fosters innovation as team members encounter new approaches and expertise.

Example: Organize monthly "collaboration sessions" where teams from marketing, product, and customer service share updates and brainstorm shared goals.

Rotate team members across functions
Rotation programs allow employees to experience different roles within the organization, enhancing their understanding of various functions and processes. This helps teams work more cohesively and appreciate the challenges faced by other departments.

Example: Have a team member from sales spend a week with the product development team to understand the product lifecycle and customer feedback loop.

Implement a job-shadowing program

Encourage team members to shadow colleagues in other roles to gain insights into different aspects of the organization. This can lead to better cross-functional collaboration and empathy across teams.

Example: Pair a marketing team member with a data analyst for a day, allowing them to observe how data insights are generated and applied.

Hold "curiosity workshops" or idea jams

Dedicate time for the team to brainstorm freely on projects or challenges. Structured workshops encourage creative thinking and help uncover new ideas that might not emerge during routine work discussions.

Example: Organize quarterly "idea jams" where team members spend half a day brainstorming solutions to a common problem or exploring new initiatives.

Encourage group learning sessions

Regularly schedule team learning sessions focused on relevant industry topics, skills, or trends. These sessions give team members the chance to learn and grow together, fostering a shared curiosity and collective growth.

Example: Host a monthly "lunch and learn" where team members take turns presenting on a new trend or recent training they've completed.

Create a shared "curiosity library"

Set up a shared digital or physical library with resources like books, articles, and reports that are relevant to the team's work. This shared knowledge base can spark conversations and deepen team expertise.

Example: Add industry articles, TED Talks, and ebooks to a shared folder and encourage team members to discuss what they've found interesting in meetings.

Reward collaborative experimentation
Recognize teams who take risks together, especially when they explore new methods or test unconventional solutions. Celebrating collaborative exploration reinforces a culture where curiosity is rewarded.

Example: When a team tries a new approach—even if it's not fully successful—acknowledge their effort in team meetings to show that experimentation is valued.

At the organizational level, exploration is about setting a tone of openness, adaptability, and continuous growth. When exploration is embedded in a company's values, it becomes a guiding principle that influences everything from strategy and innovation to employee engagement and retention. Organizations that encourage exploration create an environment where curiosity drives change, enabling the company to stay competitive, resilient, and forward-looking. As a leader, fostering exploration at this level not only strengthens your organization's capacity for innovation but also builds a reputation as a dynamic, people-focused workplace.

ENCOURAGING ORGANIZATIONAL EXPLORATION

Set strategic stretch goals
Define ambitious objectives that push the organization to expand its capabilities. These goals should be challenging enough to inspire curiosity and drive exploration, even if you're not sure exactly how to reach them. Clearly communicate these targets so everyone understands the purpose and vision.

Example: Set a goal to reduce your environmental footprint by 50% within five years, encouraging cross-departmental teams to brainstorm and explore sustainable solutions.

Establish a culture of experimentation and prototyping
Encourage teams to test new ideas on a small scale, creating prototypes or pilot programs in a controlled environment. This approach allows the organization to learn from successes and failures without major risks.

Example: Set up an "innovation lab" where teams can prototype new product features or processes and gather data on their effectiveness before a full-scale rollout.

Incentivize knowledge-sharing across departments
Recognize and reward employees who share insights or ideas with other teams. Cross-functional collaboration fosters a shared understanding of the organization's goals and broadens everyone's perspective.

Example: Implement a monthly knowledge-sharing award recognizing employees who contribute valuable insights across departments, such as finance sharing data trends with marketing.

Create an exploration fund for department initiatives
Allocate a budget for departments to pursue exploratory projects or attend industry events that can generate new ideas. This demonstrates an investment in curiosity and innovation at the organizational level.

Example: Allow each department an annual budget to fund exploration activities, like sending a team to a leading conference in their field or initiating a research project on emerging trends.

Encourage cross-functional project teams
Form project teams with members from different departments to tackle complex challenges, ensuring a diversity of perspectives and expertise. This promotes exploration beyond standard job roles and enhances organizational learning.

Example: Assign a team with members from marketing, engineering, and customer service to collaborate on improving the customer onboarding process.

Host company-wide innovation days
Set aside time each quarter for employees across all levels to come together, brainstorm, and pitch ideas for potential projects or improvements. Innovation days emphasize exploration as a core organizational value and encourage new perspectives.

Example: Hold quarterly "innovation days" where employees pitch ideas, and top ideas receive support for a pilot phase.

Promote leadership transparency and accessibility
When leaders are open about their learning experiences

and explorations, it normalizes curiosity as a strength rather than a risk. Leadership transparency fosters an environment where exploration is not only permitted but celebrated.

Example: Leaders can share insights from their professional development efforts, such as books they're reading or industry trends they're exploring, to model continuous learning.

Embed curiosity in organizational values
Include curiosity and exploration as core values in the organization's mission and vision statements. This formal commitment signals to everyone that the company values learning and adaptation as essential to its success.

Example: Add "Continuous Learning and Exploration" as a pillar in the company values, and refer to it in performance reviews and strategic discussions.

Implement open idea submissions and feedback loops
Provide platforms for employees to submit ideas and receive feedback, such as an internal suggestion portal or regular "town hall" meetings. Open channels for feedback encourage exploration by making employees feel heard and valued.

Example: Set up an online suggestion board where employees can post ideas and receive constructive feedback from leaders or peers.

Offer training and development programs focused on exploration
Develop programs that train employees in skills like creative problem-solving, design thinking, and innovation man-

agement. These programs equip individuals with tools that reinforce the organization's commitment to exploration.

Example: Offer courses on design thinking or agile methodologies to help employees approach challenges with a mindset geared toward exploration.

By encouraging exploration at the individual, team, and organizational levels, you, as a leader, are creating a culture where curiosity is valued at every level. Supporting exploration helps your organization become more innovative, resilient, and adaptable, empowering employees to engage fully and think expansively. On an individual level, exploration enhances engagement and skill-building; at the team level, it fosters collaboration and trust; and at the organizational level, it drives strategic growth and adaptability. As a leader, championing exploration not only strengthens your team's capacity to adapt and innovate but also establishes your organization as a dynamic, forward-looking place where employees feel motivated to contribute their best ideas and embrace continuous growth.

How curious are you? To find out, use the QR code in the Resources section to take the assessment.

Curiosity Reflection

Reflect on your organization's current approach to exploration:

- ☐ Do you feel that curiosity is actively encouraged at the individual, team, and organizational levels?

- ☐ Where do you see opportunities for greater exploration, and how might you contribute to fostering it?

Think about a time when you were encouraged to explore a new idea or approach in your work:

- ☐ What support did you receive, and how did it impact the outcome?

- ☐ How might you replicate or extend that encouragement to others on your team?

Consider your role in fostering psychological safety within your team:

- ☐ What actions have you taken to ensure team members feel comfortable sharing ideas and asking questions?

- ☐ How might you strengthen this environment to support more robust team exploration?

**Reflect on your organization's
willingness to experiment and prototype new ideas:**

- ☐ Are there established practices for testing ideas in a low-risk way? If not, what might you introduce to create a culture of experimentation?

- ☐ How could you support your team in adopting a mindset where learning from both success and failure is valued?

**Think about your organization's
openness to cross-functional collaboration:**

- ☐ How frequently do employees from different departments collaborate, and how could these interactions be expanded?

- ☐ What new perspectives or ideas could be gained from increased cross-departmental work?

Consider your growth as a leader in promoting exploration:

- ☐ In what ways do you model curiosity and exploration for your team?

- ☐ What steps can you take to encourage exploration as a core organizational value and part of your leadership style?

Reflect on the benefits of exploration for your organization as a whole:

- How do you think fostering exploration could contribute to your organization's adaptability and resilience?

- How might encouraging exploration help attract and retain top talent and promote innovation?

Imagine the impact of a formal exploration initiative, like an innovation day or curiosity budget, in your organization:

- How could such initiatives make a difference in team dynamics and overall organizational growth?

- What resources or structures would be needed to implement these ideas effectively?

6

FOCUSED ENGAGEMENT

Focused engagement is more than simply being busy or productive—it's about channeling your curiosity into meaningful work with undivided attention.

For individuals, this means cultivating habits and mindsets that enable you to immerse yourself in tasks, explore challenges deeply, and sustain focus over time. This level of engagement not only enhances personal performance but also builds the foundation for curiosity-driven innovation.

At the team level, focused engagement fosters collaboration, trust, and collective problem-solving. Teams that embrace curiosity work with a shared sense of purpose, exchanging ideas openly and staying present in discussions. This deep engagement fuels creativity and accelerates progress toward meaningful goals.

At the organizational level, focused engagement shapes workplace culture, driving alignment between vision, strategy, and execution. Companies that prioritize this mindset create environments where employees feel empowered to contribute, challenge assumptions, and pursue ambitious ideas with sustained effort. A culture of focus and curiosity leads to greater innovation, stronger leadership, and long-term success.

In this chapter, we take a closer look at how focused engagement operates at each of these levels—individual, team, and organization—and explore ways to cultivate it effectively.

FOCUSED ENGAGEMENT AT THE INDIVIDUAL LEVEL

When individuals master focused engagement, they unlock a greater sense of purpose and satisfaction in their work. It's the difference between going through the motions and becoming fully present in what you do. In a world filled with distractions, fostering focused engagement allows you to dive into your work with intention, creativity, and clarity.

Why Focused Engagement Matters

At its core, focused engagement amplifies curiosity. It enables you to direct your inquisitiveness toward solving problems, learning new skills, or uncovering opportunities for growth.

Research indicates that employee engagement is closely linked to job satisfaction and performance. For instance, a study published in the *Journal of Human Services* found that employee engagement has a statistical relationship with job satisfaction, commitment, job involvement, and task performance productivity.[1]

Additionally, Gallup's research highlights that organizations focusing on employee engagement can improve business outcomes, including profitability and productivity.[2]

By immersing yourself in tasks and maintaining focused engagement, you can enhance your problem-solving abilities, deepen your understanding, and foster personal growth, all of which contribute to higher job satisfaction and goal achievement.

> Focused engagement transforms scattered curiosity into purposeful action.

Research shows that people who are highly engaged in their work report higher levels of job satisfaction and are more likely to achieve their goals.[3] For individuals, focused engagement leads to:

1. **Deeper Understanding**

    By immersing yourself in a task, you allow curiosity to drive deeper exploration. This leads to insights and solutions that might otherwise remain undiscovered.

2. **Enhanced Problem-Solving**

    Focused engagement sharpens your ability to tackle complex problems. With full attention, you can approach challenges creatively and methodically.

3. **Increased Resilience**

    Being fully engaged helps you persist through obstacles. When curiosity and focus align, you're more likely to stay motivated and overcome setbacks.

4. **Personal Growth**
   Immersion in meaningful tasks fosters skill development and builds confidence in your ability to take on new challenges.

Strategies for Building Focused Engagement

Focused engagement doesn't happen by chance—it requires intentional effort and the right strategies to cultivate it. Ron Ricci, a senior executive at Cisco, experienced one of the most transformative moments of his career through focused engagement. At the time, he had transitioned from a leadership role into a sales operations position—only to find himself unexpectedly responsible for a $75 million budget and a team of 200 technical engineers, most of whom spoke a language of microservices, hypervisors, and virtual machines that he didn't yet understand.

Rather than retreat, Ron leaned into curiosity. He immersed himself in their world, traveling to Cisco's proof-of-concept lab to learn directly from the engineers. His genuine willingness to engage deeply earned their trust, unlocking insights that ultimately led to a $500 million investment in building the world's largest demonstration cloud. This innovation allowed Cisco's global sales teams to demonstrate products in real-time from anywhere in the world, accelerating sales cycles, improving customer confidence, and driving multimillion-dollar revenue growth.

That experience didn't just redefine his role at Cisco—it shaped the next chapter of his career, equipping him to lead in software entrepreneurship and venture-backed startups. This story proves that curiosity, when paired with deep engagement, can drive extraordinary transformation—both personally and organizationally.[4]

By developing habits that support deep focus and sustained attention, you can harness curiosity as a driving force for productivity and innovation. The following are practical strategies to help you strengthen your ability to engage fully in your work.

1. **Start with Curiosity**
   Approach every task with a sense of curiosity. Ask yourself: "What can I learn from this?" or "How can this contribute to my growth or understanding?" Shifting your mindset from obligation to opportunity helps you connect more deeply with your work.

2. **Eliminate Distractions**
   Identify and remove common distractions that pull your attention away. Whether it's turning off notifications, creating a dedicated workspace, or setting specific focus periods, removing interruptions allows you to stay immersed in the task at hand.

3. **Use Time-Blocking**
   Schedule blocks of uninterrupted time for your most important tasks. During these periods, commit to deep work, resisting the urge to multitask or shift focus.

4. **Set Clear Intentions**
   Begin each task with a clear understanding of your goal. Having a specific intention channels your curiosity and energy toward a purposeful outcome.

5. **Practice Mindfulness**
   Incorporate mindfulness techniques to stay present in the moment. Brief mindfulness exercises, such as deep breathing or a five-minute meditation, can help reset your focus and calm your mind.

6. **Embrace the Flow State**
   Aim to enter the flow state, where you're fully immersed and energized by your work. This happens when tasks are challenging enough to engage your skills but not so overwhelming that they cause frustration.

7. **Celebrate Small Wins**
   Acknowledge and celebrate progress, even on small milestones. Recognizing achievements fuels motivation and reinforces your commitment to focused engagement.

Examples of Focused Engagement

A project manager tackling complexity
Imagine a project manager faced with a tight deadline for a new product launch. Instead of being overwhelmed by the magnitude of the task, they break it into manageable components, blocking time to address each piece with focused attention. By eliminating distractions and staying present, they not only meet the deadline but also uncover opportunities to streamline future projects.

A designer exploring creativity
A graphic designer working on a challenging campaign embraces curiosity by experimenting with bold, unconventional ideas. By fully immersing themselves in the creative process— free from distractions—they produce designs that exceed expectations and spark excitement.

A new employee building skills
A recent hire in a tech firm dedicates focused time each day

to learning a coding language. With a clear goal and curiosity-driven approach, they make steady progress, eventually contributing new insights to their team.

The Impact of Focused Engagement

Focused engagement at the individual level doesn't just improve performance—it transforms how we approach our work. When we immerse ourselves in curiosity, we feel more connected to our tasks and more confident in our ability to make an impact.

This kind of engagement inspires others as well. A leader who models focused engagement sets the tone for their team, demonstrating that curiosity and presence are valuable traits. Similarly, an employee who approaches their work with deep focus uplifts the culture around them, showing colleagues what's possible when distractions are replaced with dedication.

> Curiosity without focus is a spark without fuel.

In the end, focused engagement is a personal practice that has ripple effects across teams and organizations. It's a reminder that our best work happens when curiosity drives us to dig deeper, think smarter, and stay fully present in the moment. By cultivating this habit, you set the stage for growth, innovation, and fulfillment in everything you do.

FOCUSED ENGAGEMENT AT THE TEAM LEVEL

Focused engagement goes beyond mere engagement—it means immersing yourself in your work with undivided attention. This type of focus is crucial for channeling curiosity effectively and getting to the heart of complex challenges.

In 2008, just as the financial crisis was unfolding, Mike Cunnion joined Remedy Health Media (then named Medizine), a digital platform for people with chronic illnesses, as its new president. He was brought on to lead a turnaround, including a carefully planned expansion, amid the economic turbulence. One of his first challenges involved acquiring another health information company that had capabilities Remedy needed and double the employees, but had yet to achieve consistent profitability. The deal closed in early December 2012, and with it came the uncomfortable reality that around 35% of the staff would likely be laid off just before the holidays.

As Mike tells it, the two companies had previously been rivals, with both exploring acquisition opportunities. Remedy, however, had maintained a more focused approach, which ultimately left it in a stronger financial position. "They had made a lot of bets and had made modest progress on all of them," Mike says. "Ultimately, we were buying a company that was much larger than us but struggling."[5]

In mergers and acquisitions, the typical approach is to integrate valuable assets, cut the remaining ones, lay off staff from the acquired company, and quickly align operations to hit financial targets. Remedy's deal was backed by private equity, and investors are not typically focused on retaining continuity among the incoming staff.

But Mike was curious. The people at the acquired company were talented and collaborative, and he saw potential to leverage their skills in building a unified culture. "Key people coming in were wondering how big their teams would be and who they'd report to," he recalls. "I was wondering what we could do to get a jump start on solidifying the culture of a combined organization."

Mike held a joint team-building session with both companies' senior leadership just before the acquisition was finalized—a bold move, given that many roles were still unsettled. Some Remedy executives questioned whether it was wise to spend a full day on team building, especially with so many financial and operational details in flux. But Mike's focused engagement made all the difference: The session established a shared culture from the start, helping employees feel valued and involved in the process.

"It allowed the new people to see that we cared about culture and collaboration," Mike says. "It wasn't a 'winner versus loser' situation—it was a combined effort." Although layoffs still occurred, Remedy retained about half of the incoming company's top executives, showing a commitment to integrating talent rather than simply acquiring assets.

Patagonia's "Don't Buy This Jacket" campaign is a notable example of focused engagement within a company. Launched on Black Friday in 2011, the campaign featured a full-page advertisement in the *New York Times* urging consumers to consider the environmental impact of their purchases and to buy only what they need. This initiative was part of Patagonia's Common Threads program, which aimed to reduce unnecessary consumption by encouraging customers to repair, reuse, and recycle products.

The development of this campaign involved collaboration across various departments within Patagonia. Employees from marketing, retail, and other areas provided input to ensure the message aligned with the company's environmental values. This collective effort required team members to fully commit to the mission, even as it challenged traditional marketing strategies. The result was a campaign that not only resonated with consumers but also strengthened Patagonia's brand and deepened its culture of environmental stewardship.[6]

In both examples, focused engagement created a bridge between curiosity and concrete results, allowing leaders to maintain purpose and cohesion during times of change. By fostering focused engagement, leaders empower their teams to bring their full attention and talents to the work at hand. This level of immersion helps organizations address challenges, sustain innovation, and develop a resilient culture capable of thriving amid disruption.

By practicing focused engagement, you as a leader create an environment where curiosity drives progress and unity, and where every team member feels invested in the shared journey toward success.

ENCOURAGING FOCUSED ENGAGEMENT AT THE TEAM LEVEL: HOST TEAM TASK

Prioritization workshops

Run workshops that teach prioritization techniques, like the Eisenhower Matrix, to help the team collectively decide which tasks are most critical. This strengthens team focus by aligning everyone on high-impact activities.

Example: Conduct a quarterly workshop where the team discusses and categorizes upcoming tasks, aligning on what's most important for the group's success.

Establish team focus hours

Designate specific hours when the entire team is encouraged to work on priority projects without interruptions. Shared focus hours allow the team to align on collective goals while minimizing distractions.

Example: Set aside 10 a.m. to 12 p.m. as "focus hours" twice a week, when team members know to avoid meetings and concentrate on key projects.

Foster a single-tasking culture
Encourage the team to adopt single-tasking practices, emphasizing the quality and depth of focusing on one task at a time. Recognize team achievements that result from single-tasking efforts.

Example: Share examples in team meetings of successful single-tasked projects to model the importance of undivided attention.

Define clear, meaningful team goals
Set goals that resonate with the team's values and align with overall organizational objectives. When team goals are clear and purposeful, members stay more engaged and committed.

Example: In monthly team check-ins, discuss how the team's goals connect to the organization's mission and acknowledge the team's progress.

Conduct start, stop, and continue team exercises
Regularly assess tasks and projects as a group to identify what to start, stop, or continue. This helps the team focus on high-value activities and collectively eliminate low-impact tasks.

Example: At the start of each quarter, hold a session where the team evaluates ongoing projects and agrees on tasks to discontinue, refine, or expand.

Encourage team reflections on focus
Prompt the team to reflect on shared priorities and adjust goals as needed. Team reflections reinforce alignment and help everyone maintain focus on collective objectives.

Example: In weekly team meetings, prompt a brief discussion on what went well, what could improve, and how to maintain focus on upcoming priorities.

Provide training in collaborative time management tools
Offer training on tools like Trello, Asana, or Microsoft Teams to help the team stay organized and aligned on tasks. This empowers them to collectively manage time and workflows effectively.

Example: Hold monthly sessions where team members share tips on using time management tools for team projects and collaboration.

Implement team sprint intervals for high-impact work
Use focused, time-boxed "sprint" intervals for group projects to drive productivity and build a shared sense of accomplishment. These sprints help the team immerse deeply in a project together.

Example: Plan a two-hour team sprint each week for high-priority projects, followed by a quick debrief on progress and next steps.

Encourage mindfulness breaks for the team
Support short, mindful breaks for the team to recharge and refresh their collective focus. Mindful pauses as a group can improve overall engagement and mental clarity.

Example: Add a mindful minute before or after team meetings, encouraging everyone to take a few deep breaths and reset their focus.

Set team expectations for communication response times
Agree as a team on reasonable response times for emails and messages. This allows everyone to concentrate on priority tasks without the pressure of constant notifications.

Example: Establish a team agreement that emails received in the morning can be addressed after "focus hours" to allow everyone time for uninterrupted work.

FOCUSED ENGAGEMENT AT THE ORGANIZATION LEVEL

At the organizational level, fostering focused engagement means creating an environment where employees can concentrate on high-impact work without unnecessary distractions. When focus is prioritized across the organization, productivity, innovation, and job satisfaction all improve. A culture of focused engagement encourages employees to immerse themselves in meaningful work, leading to more consistent progress toward organizational goals and enhancing overall resilience.

Here are some actionable strategies to promote focused engagement across the organization:

Designate quiet zones
Establish designated quiet zones in the office where employees can work without interruptions. These areas signal that focused work is valued and respected across the organization.

Example: Create "focus booths" or quiet workspaces that employees can reserve when they need undisturbed time to concentrate on critical projects.

Implement "no-meeting" days

Designate specific days as "no-meeting" days to allow employees uninterrupted time for deep work. This fosters focused engagement by giving everyone time to dive into complex tasks without the distraction of meetings.

Example: Make Wednesdays meeting-free to encourage all employees to focus on priority projects and tasks that require concentration.

Offer flexibility for personalized focus times

Allow employees to set their own "focus hours" based on their peak productivity times, with clear communication on availability. Flexibility supports focused engagement by aligning work hours with personal rhythms.

Example: Encourage teams to share preferred "focus hours" with colleagues, allowing everyone to plan around each other's high-focus times.

Integrate mindfulness and focus training

Provide training sessions on mindfulness and techniques for improving focus. Teaching employees how to manage distractions and stay engaged supports both individual and collective productivity.

Example: Host monthly workshops on mindfulness, time management, and focus under pressure, equipping employees with practical strategies.

Promote task batching for teams and departments
Encourage teams to "batch" similar tasks together to minimize switching between unrelated tasks. Task batching streamlines workflows, improving overall focus and reducing time lost to distractions.

Example: Schedule specific days for tasks like administrative work, team planning, or creative brainstorming, allowing teams to focus on one type of task at a time.

Leverage project management tools for clarity
Use project management tools like Asana, Monday, or Trello to clarify project timelines, responsibilities, and deadlines. Clear workflows allow employees to focus on tasks without the uncertainty of disorganized processes.

Example: Set up a project board where each team member's responsibilities are clear, helping them focus on their contributions without distractions.

Encourage "digital detox" practices
Promote periods of "digital detox" during the workday when employees can step away from screens and reduce mental fatigue. These breaks can improve attention and re-energize employees for high-focus tasks.

Example: Offer a "tech-free" room where employees can take screen-free breaks to reset their focus before returning to work.

Establish organization-wide communication protocols
Create and communicate organization-wide guidelines for response times on emails, messages, and calls. Clarity around expected response times helps employees focus on tasks without feeling pressure to respond immediately.

Example: Set an organizational standard that emails should be responded to within 24 hours, freeing employees to engage deeply with their current work without constant interruptions.

Invest in ergonomic, focus-friendly workspaces
Design office spaces to optimize focus and comfort, using ergonomic furniture, adjustable lighting, and noise control. A well-designed workspace helps employees maintain focus and physical well-being during long periods of work.

Example: Equip each workstation with ergonomic chairs and adjustable monitors and use soundproofing panels to minimize office noise.

Recognize and reward focused achievements
Create recognition programs that celebrate employees who demonstrate focused engagement in achieving significant goals. Highlighting these efforts reinforces a culture where focus and dedication are valued.

Example: During quarterly meetings, recognize team members who completed high-focus projects, demonstrating the value of immersion in impactful work.

Focused engagement is transformative for individuals and organizations alike. By fostering this at every level, from quiet spaces for individual focus to organization-wide practices that reduce distractions, you create an environment where employees can deeply immerse themselves in meaningful work. Focused engagement enhances productivity, drives innovation, and strengthens team morale, creating a resilient organization capable of tackling challenges effectively.

As a leader, promoting focused engagement not only empowers your team to perform at their best but also sends a clear message that quality work matters. An organization that values focused engagement becomes more agile, achieving its goals with clarity and purpose. Supporting focus at the organizational level enables employees to connect with their work deeply and, in turn, fosters a stronger sense of purpose, satisfaction, and growth.

Curiosity Reflection

Reflect on a time when you felt fully engaged in your work:

- ☐ What specific factors or environment contributed to your sense of focus?

- ☐ How might you recreate these conditions to sustain focused engagement in your current role?

Think about the biggest distractions that disrupt your team's focus:

- ☐ What practical changes could reduce these distractions?

- ☐ How could you support your team in adopting practices that improve collective focus?

Consider the role of clear goals in fostering focus within your organization:

- ☐ How well do current goals align with the team's values and sense of purpose?

- ☐ What changes could you make to ensure goals are meaningful and support focused engagement?

Reflect on your current workspace environment:

- ☐ Does the workspace support focused work, or does it create distractions?

- ☐ What improvements could be made to create a more focus-friendly environment for your team?

Think about how communication protocols affect focus:

- ☐ Are there expectations for immediate responses that disrupt focus?

- ☐ How might adjusting communication norms improve both focus and productivity?

Reflect on your role in modeling focused engagement for your team:

- ☐ How do your actions demonstrate the importance of focused, high-quality work?

- ☐ What steps could you take to lead by example and foster focused engagement within the team?

7
INSPIRATIONAL CREATIVITY

Inspirational creativity is the practice of fostering an environment where imagination, fresh perspectives, and resourcefulness are encouraged and actively supported. Unlike creativity that focuses solely on solving immediate problems, inspirational creativity invites people to think beyond the usual constraints, sparking innovative ideas and energizing teams toward new possibilities. It involves creating a culture where employees feel empowered to ask "what if" questions, reimagine traditional approaches, and pursue ideas that may initially seem unconventional.

In a workplace with inspirational creativity, employees at all levels feel motivated to think expansively, knowing their ideas are valued and their contributions make a difference. Leaders play a key role in setting this tone by encouraging risk-taking, celebrating diverse perspectives, and creating space for exploration. Interestingly, our June 2025 research revealed a surprising pattern: professionals with higher levels of education reported lower scores in Inspirational Creativity.[1] One possible explanation? These individuals may have higher expectations for creativity in their environments—and may rate their organizations more critically when that support isn't present. Meaning innovation isn't just about generating new ideas—it's about ensuring that even your most experienced people feel inspired to contribute them.

> Inspirational creativity is the alchemy of connecting ideas in new and surprising ways.

The result is a more engaged and dynamic team, capable of approaching challenges in inventive ways that fuel long-term organizational growth and adaptability. Inspirational creativity can transform ordinary tasks into powerful moments of insight and innovation, making work more meaningful and positioning an organization to thrive.

INSPIRING CREATIVITY IN INDIVIDUALS

As a leader, fostering creativity in individuals involves giving employees space and encouragement to pursue their ideas. This boosts their confidence, resourcefulness, and capacity for innovative thinking, ultimately contributing to the organization's growth.

Encourage creative skill development
Support employees in building skills that fuel creativity, such as design thinking, creative writing, or storytelling. Offering creative skill development shows that the organization values growth and imaginative thinking.

Example: Provide access to online courses or workshops in creativity-related fields and encourage employees to share their learnings with the team.

Set up a "curiosity corner" for exploration resources
Curate a collection of creative resources—books, articles, or podcasts—that employees can access to spark inspiration and expand their perspectives.

Example: Create a digital "curiosity corner" with resources like TED Talks, articles, or industry reports, and encourage employees to contribute their own discoveries.

Celebrate individual achievements in innovation
Recognize employees who take creative approaches to problem-solving. This motivates others to explore their own innovative ideas.

Example: Highlight an "Innovator of the Month" who has demonstrated resourcefulness or creativity, and share their contributions with the organization.

Encourage diverse learning experiences
Encourage employees to attend conferences or take part in industry events that can inspire fresh ideas. Exposure to new trends broadens perspectives and fosters creativity.

Example: Provide stipends or days off to attend workshops or conferences, where employees can explore innovative concepts and bring insights back to their teams.

INSPIRING CREATIVITY IN TEAMS

> Curiosity gives leaders permission to experiment and embrace imperfect first drafts.

Encouraging creativity within teams requires fostering an environment where collaboration, experimentation, and open-mindedness are valued. Team-based creativity strengthens problem-solving abilities and enhances project outcomes.

Conduct regular innovation workshops
Host workshops focused on creative exercises and brainstorming sessions to generate fresh ideas. These sessions create a collaborative space for team members to explore new approaches together.

Example: Hold quarterly innovation workshops where teams brainstorm on strategic issues, fostering a culture of collective problem-solving.

Use design thinking techniques
Encourage design thinking as a structured approach to problem-solving, guiding teams through stages of empathizing, defining, ideating, prototyping, and testing solutions.

Example: Organize a design-thinking workshop where team members identify customer pain points and prototype solutions, stimulating empathy and innovation.

Organize hackathons or innovation challenges

Host internal hackathons or innovation challenges where teams work intensively to solve specific problems, promoting collaboration and rapid idea generation.

Example: Set up a 48-hour hackathon for teams to develop solutions to a business challenge, with a prize for the most innovative idea.

Foster open storytelling sessions

Encourage team members to share stories of past projects, highlighting successes, lessons learned, and creative approaches. This builds trust and opens minds to new possibilities.

Example: Implement bi-monthly storytelling sessions where team members share insights from recent projects, inspiring others to think creatively.

Embrace a prototyping mindset

Encourage teams to create quick prototypes to test ideas before full-scale implementation. This allows for rapid experimentation and iterative improvement.

Example: Introduce a "Prototype Day" when teams work on basic models or mockups, refining ideas through feedback.

Reward creative problem-solving

Recognize and celebrate creative approaches to challenges. Celebrating team members who think outside the box reinforces a culture of innovative problem-solving.

Example: Implement a "Creative Solution Award" for teams that approach a challenge in an inventive way, recognizing their contribution to the organization's goals.

INSPIRING CREATIVITY IN ORGANIZATIONS

At the organizational level, a culture of inspirational creativity promotes long-term innovation, adaptability, and resilience. When creativity is embedded as a core value, the organization thrives by continually adapting to changes and seizing new opportunities.

Design flexible, inspiring workspaces
Create workspaces with comfortable seating, writable surfaces, and other creative elements to inspire brainstorming and spontaneous idea-sharing.

Example: Designate collaborative "creativity zones" with whiteboards and flexible seating, encouraging teams to gather for impromptu brainstorming.

Promote diversity and inclusion initiatives
Encourage diverse perspectives by actively hiring from various backgrounds and creating inclusive spaces. Diverse teams often bring richer, more innovative solutions.

Example: Develop mentorship programs that connect employees across different departments, promoting a diversity of perspectives in problem-solving.

Support learning from failures with after-action reviews
Conduct after-action reviews that frame failures as learning opportunities, showing employees that taking risks is part of the innovation process.

Example: After a project, hold a "lessons learned" session to discuss what worked and what didn't, with an emphasis on how to improve future initiatives.

Launch an "ideas portal" for employees

Create an internal platform where employees can submit ideas for improving processes or creating new products. This builds an inclusive culture where everyone's creativity is valued.

Example: Establish a company-wide ideas portal where employees can post suggestions, with monthly reviews and rewards for high-potential ideas.

Develop recognition programs for innovation

Celebrate innovative ideas and achievements through recognition programs. Highlighting creativity shows that the organization values fresh thinking at all levels.

Example: Hold an annual "Innovation Awards" ceremony that honors teams and individuals who bring forward impactful, creative solutions.

Inspirational creativity is the driving force behind organizational resilience and adaptability. By creating an environment where employees feel encouraged to think outside the box, leaders cultivate a culture where imagination and resourcefulness flourish. From individual exploration to team brainstorming sessions and organization-wide recognition programs, fostering creativity at every level not only sparks innovation but also instills a sense of purpose and excitement in the workplace.

As a leader, encouraging inspirational creativity allows you to unlock your team's potential and steer your organization toward long-term success. In a culture that values creativity, employees are more motivated, engaged, and likely to bring innovative solutions to complex challenges. Inspirational creativity builds a legacy of growth and adaptability, positioning your organization to thrive well into the future.

Curiosity Reflection

Reflect on a time when you felt encouraged to be creative in your work:

- ☐ What support or conditions made you feel free to explore new ideas?

- ☐ How might you recreate or extend these conditions to inspire others?

Consider how you currently foster creativity in your team:

- ☐ Are there specific practices or policies that encourage your team to think outside the box?

- ☐ What additional steps could you take to support and celebrate creative thinking?

Think about the role of diversity in creativity:

- ☐ How do diverse perspectives in your team contribute to innovative solutions?

- [ ] What steps could you take to ensure diverse voices are heard and valued in creative processes?

Reflect on how failures are handled within your organization:

- [ ] Are failures seen as learning opportunities, or do they stifle creativity and risk-taking?

- [ ] What could you do to create a safe environment where employees feel encouraged to take risks?

Consider a recent challenge that required creativity:

- [ ] What specific actions helped you or your team approach this challenge innovatively?

- [ ] How can you apply these actions to future projects to foster an ongoing culture of creativity?

8
OPENNESS TO NEW IDEAS

All of the factors just covered—exploration, focused engagement, and inspirational creativity—can only work when your organization is actually open to receiving new ideas and ensuring that the best ones are implemented. In other words, it's important that curiosity is not just given lip service; it has to be put into action. Openness to new ideas may be the most high-leverage aspect of all four factors of curiosity.

When Dr. Joan Kelly had to figure out a way to move patients through a hospital during the COVID-19 pandemic, she looked outside of healthcare for inspiration, drawing on systems used by airlines to board passengers. Dr. Kelly was chief experience officer at Yale New Haven Health System during the onset of the pandemic. She and her colleagues faced rapid-fire decisions, juggling a deadly new virus, shortages, and overloaded hospital systems. Normally, healthcare professionals base their decisions on evidence and clear guidelines, but COVID-19 demanded they make decisions on the fly, often without precedent.

"We follow evidence-based rules and foundations of quality and safety," Dr. Kelly explained. "And was it done before, and is it peer-reviewed?"[1] But during COVID-19, they had to improvise quickly. They set up screening, testing, and safety systems without a clear roadmap and needed to secure clinics and hospital rooms, all while managing limited resources.

Dr. Kelly and her team recognized that they had to be open to ideas from outside their field to stay ahead of the virus. One such idea came from the airline industry. Facing long lines for testing and treatment, Dr. Kelly had one of her staff members call the airlines to understand their strategies for moving people efficiently. Applying this method to the hospital setting reduced cycle time, allowing them to treat two to three times as many patients. When they faced issues like calibrating face recognition on iPads for patients wearing masks or improving recognition accuracy across diverse skin tones, they turned to Yale's tech labs and recruited medical students to rapidly develop solutions.[2]

> Openness means considering ideas that challenge your own beliefs.

Openness to new ideas proved essential, not just in process

innovations but in empowering staff to think creatively. Dr. Kelly saw that her team's ability to innovate was tied to confidence in their ideas. "One of them said to me, 'I never thought we could even call an airline. Who's going to answer?' I thought, well, you don't know until you try." Over time, staff who were used to staying within defined roles were able to embrace the creativity needed to keep people safe. They shared resources, recruited support from other departments, and even adopted a "buddy system" borrowed from the Army, pairing team members to check in on each other's well-being.

A similar example of openness to external ideas can be seen in Starbucks's transformation under CEO Howard Schultz, which changed the company from a coffee bean retailer into a community-centered coffeehouse. Schultz was inspired by Italian espresso bars, where he noticed the social atmosphere around coffee—a stark contrast to the transactional approach of coffee shops in the US. When he proposed this model to Starbucks's original founders, they initially resisted, not seeing the value of a "third place" where people could gather outside of work and home. However, Schultz's curiosity and persistence led to Starbucks adopting his vision, transforming the brand and pioneering a new coffee culture that would influence the entire industry.

These anecdotes show that openness to new ideas can lead to transformative change. Both Dr. Joan Kelly's team and Schultz's Starbucks gained strength by looking outside their usual boundaries, inviting fresh insights that would shape their futures. An interesting pattern emerged in our June 2025 analysis of 394 professionals across industries: scores for Openness to New Ideas increased with both age and education level.[3] This suggests that lived experience may broaden one's perspective, leading to a greater willingness to consider alternative viewpoints. Meaning organizations benefit when they create space for multigenerational voices and encourage lifelong learning. Openness isn't just a mindset—it's a muscle that strengthens over time.

FOSTERING OPENNESS TO NEW IDEAS

Curiosity leads people to seek out new experiences, ideas, and challenges. The ability to do this—to expand knowledge and foster adaptability—is a key trait of a curious and agile individual. It's important for organizational leaders to create an environment that values openness. In such an organization, you'll see people taking every opportunity to listen to others from diverse backgrounds. Ideas are valued, even when they diverge from the prevailing norms or conventional wisdom. Leaders who cultivate openness encourage curiosity, which leads to creative problem-solving and innovation.

> The most innovative organizations create space for disagreement and discovery.

For example, Henry Ford famously borrowed his assembly line model from the overhead trolley system used in meatpacking plants. Similarly, IKEA took inspiration from an unexpected source: Flat-pack furniture emerged when an IKEA employee observed a colleague removing the legs from a table to fit it into a car. This simple act of curiosity led to a defining feature of IKEA's product line and set a new standard for efficient, user-friendly furniture packaging. Like Ford and IKEA, organizations that look beyond their immediate industry for inspiration gain the flexibility to innovate and adapt.

OPENNESS TO NEW IDEAS AT THE INDIVIDUAL LEVEL

Supporting openness to new ideas at the individual level allows employees to broaden their perspectives, gain new skills, and feel more engaged in their work. Here are specific ways to encourage this:

Attend networking events

Encourage employees to attend industry events, meetups, or conferences. Networking with others outside their usual circles exposes them to new perspectives and fosters openness.

Example: Support each team member in attending one industry event per quarter to share and discuss new ideas with their colleagues afterward.

Support travel and cross-cultural experiences

Encourage employees to explore new locations and cultures by attending global conferences or participating in exchange programs. Experiencing diverse perspectives firsthand inspires new ways of thinking.

Example: Offer stipends for employees to attend international conferences or training, where they can gain insights from other markets and cultures.

Encourage lifelong learning

Provide resources for employees to pursue courses, certifications, or training in areas outside their immediate roles. Expanding knowledge beyond their primary expertise sparks curiosity and new approaches.

Example: Offer reimbursements for courses on platforms like Coursera or Udemy and encourage employees to share what they learned with the team.

Incorporate regular reflection practices

Encourage employees to set aside time for self-reflection on their goals, challenges, and areas for growth. Reflection fosters curiosity and receptivity to new ideas.

Example: Introduce a weekly reflection hour when employees can evaluate their recent work and identify areas for growth.

Read outside your field

Promote reading or listening to books, podcasts, and articles outside employees' primary expertise. Exposure to diverse subjects broadens perspectives and fosters creative connections.

Example: Host quarterly reading days when employees can spend time reading a book of their choice and share a new insight during a team meeting.

Openness to new ideas is essential for creating a culture where exploration, focused engagement, and inspirational creativity can thrive. When an organization truly embraces new perspectives, it enables employees to approach challenges resourcefully and collaboratively. An open culture not only encourages curiosity but also drives growth, adaptability, and resilience, creating an environment where innovative thinking can flourish.

As a leader, fostering openness to new ideas enables your team to engage fully and bring forward fresh perspectives that may lead to transformative solutions. By creating pathways for ideas to be shared, valued, and implemented, you position your organization to continually learn, grow, and lead in a changing world.

Curiosity Reflection

- ☐ When was the last time you actively sought inspiration from outside your industry? What did you learn, and how did it shape your thinking?

- ☐ How does your organization respond to new or unconventional ideas? Are they welcomed, tested, and explored, or dismissed too quickly?

- ☐ What is one problem you're currently facing that could benefit from an outside perspective? Who could you reach out to for fresh insights?

- ☐ Think about a time when you resisted a new idea. What was your initial hesitation, and in hindsight, was it valid? How could you approach similar situations with more openness?

- ☐ How do you encourage curiosity within your team or organization? What practices or behaviors can you implement to make openness to new ideas a norm rather than an exception?

- ☐ What is one industry, book, or podcast outside your expertise that you could explore this month? How might this new perspective influence your approach to work?

- ☐ Are you creating space for reflection and idea-sharing in your daily or weekly routine? If not, how can you build in time to capture new insights and consider fresh perspectives?

- ☐ Encouraging openness to new ideas doesn't just spark innovation—it strengthens adaptability, fuels collaboration, and helps organizations stay ahead of change. How will you cultivate it in your own work?

Conclusion

THE FUTURE OF CURIOSITY

As we conclude our exploration of curiosity in the workplace, it's worth taking a moment to reflect on the core principles we've covered. Curiosity is not simply a trait some possess and others don't; it's a skill that individuals, teams, and entire organizations can cultivate and refine. Through structured *exploration*, employees and teams open themselves up to learning and understanding more deeply. *Focused engagement* allows for full immersion in challenges, channeling curiosity into meaningful work. *Inspirational creativity* encourages employees to dream beyond the status quo, generating fresh perspectives that lead to innovative solutions. And perhaps most critical is *openness to new ideas*, the willingness to actually act on these fresh insights, ensuring curiosity isn't just encouraged in theory but integrated into the day-to-day workings of a company.

Each of these elements serves to fuel growth, resilience, and adaptability—qualities that are not only desirable but essential in today's workplace. A culture of curiosity allows us to respond to rapid changes with agility, rather than clinging to outdated practices. When we foster curiosity, we're creating environments where employees feel empowered to contribute their best ideas, where teams work cohesively to tackle complex challenges, and where organizations are equipped to innovate and lead in evolving industries.

> Curiosity isn't a luxury— it's a leadership necessity.

Curiosity is not innate; it is something we can nurture and develop. With conscious effort, we can build a workplace culture where curiosity thrives, regardless of individual starting points. When curiosity is cultivated, we see greater engagement, improved problem-solving, and higher job satisfaction—all of which drive organizational success.

THE IMPLICATIONS OF A CURIOUS FUTURE WORKPLACE

The impact of fostering curiosity in the workplace extends beyond individual jobs and daily tasks. It influences leadership styles, business strategies, and even the structural foundations of organizations. Leaders who embrace curiosity inspire their teams to seek knowledge, adapt to change, and approach problems with an open mind. This leads to a shift in leadership from directive to supportive, where leaders act as facilitators who nurture growth and innovation.

In terms of business strategies, curiosity opens doors to opportunities that may have gone unnoticed. Organizations that prioritize curiosity are more likely to invest in research, consider unconventional partnerships, and experiment with new products or services. In the post-pandemic workplace, where hybrid models and digital transformation have become the norm, a curious mindset enables organizations to navigate these transitions with greater ease. It allows them to remain adaptable, agile, and prepared for further changes on the horizon.

Curiosity-driven organizations also redefine their missions and values, embedding openness, adaptability, and continuous learning as pillars of their identity. This reshaping of organizational structure encourages collaboration across teams and departments, breaking down silos and promoting a culture of inclusivity. It's a move toward a more interconnected and dynamic workplace where every individual's perspective is valued and ideas flow freely. As we face a world with increasingly complex problems, a culture that fosters curiosity may be one of our greatest strengths.

> The journey to curiosity is what leads us to possibility, growth, and discovery.

A FINAL CALL TO ACTION

As you consider the role of curiosity in your life and work, think of this: Each of us has the potential to be a catalyst for curiosity. In a world of 7.9 billion people, we are here because of the curiosity of those who came before us. They dared to question, to try, to learn. They pushed boundaries, took risks, and persevered through challenges so that we might live in a world where exploration, innovation, and human connection are possible. Now it's our turn to honor that legacy by nurturing curiosity in ourselves and others.

Building a culture of curiosity isn't just about personal or organizational gain—it's about creating a future where people feel seen, heard, valued, and capable of making a difference. Let curiosity be your compass. Lead with questions, remain open to unexpected insights, and encourage those around you to do the same. Because when we build curiosity-driven organizations, we're not just shaping better workplaces; we're contributing to a more compassionate, collaborative, and innovative world. So go forward, cultivate curiosity, and watch as it transforms not only your work but the lives and communities it touches.

RESOURCES

Curiosity is a skill that we can continue to cultivate, and many tools and resources are available to support that journey. In this section, you'll find a curated list of books, TED Talks, self-assessments, and online resources to deepen your understanding of curiosity, creativity, and innovation in the workplace. These resources offer practical insights, inspiring ideas, and further opportunities to apply what you've learned here. For additional tools, articles, and updates, you can also visit my website, debraclary.com or connect with me on social media. I welcome your thoughts, questions, and insights—let's keep the conversation going!

BOOKS

The Innovator's Dilemma by Clayton Christensen
A classic on innovation, discussing how curiosity and adaptability are key in navigating disruptive technologies and market shifts.

Range: Why Generalists Triumph in a Specialized World by David Epstein
Delves into how a broad range of experiences can foster innovation and creativity, perfect for those looking to expand their curiosity across disciplines.

Originals: How Non-Conformists Move the World by Adam Grant
Investigates how to challenge the status quo with creativity, curiosity, and courage, backed by research and examples.

A Curious Mind: The Secret to a Bigger Life by Brian Grazer and Charles Fishman
Explores the role of curiosity in personal and professional success, with insights from one of Hollywood's most influential producers.

VIRTUAL TALKS

Curiosity: Two Truths & A Lie by Debra Clary (Ted Talk)
Explores how curiosity can bridge divides, foster meaningful connections, and uncover deeper truths in our relationships and conversations. It highlights the transformative power of asking questions and embracing curiosity to navigate a complex and divided world.

Grit: The Power of Passion and Perseverance by Angela Duckworth (Ted Talk)
While focused on resilience, this talk illustrates the curiosity that drives people to pursue challenging goals and overcome obstacles.

The Art of Asking by Amanda Palmer (Ted Talk)
A moving exploration of the power of asking questions and

building connections, emphasizing the importance of openness in both personal and professional realms.

The Power of Curiosity by Brian Grazer
(*Harvard Business Review* podcast: https://hbr.org/podcast/2015/04/brian-grazer-on-the-power-of-curiosity) Grazer shares how asking questions has driven his career and personal growth, offering actionable advice for anyone looking to cultivate curiosity.

SELF-ASSESSMENTS AND TOOLS

Curiosity Curve Self-Assessment
Measure your curiosity levels across various domains with this quick self-assessment, available on curiositycurve.com.

Strengths Finder by Gallup
A popular assessment to identify personal strengths, which can be a great complement to curiosity by helping you leverage your strengths in exploration and creativity (https://www.gallup.com/cliftonstrengths/en/strengthsfinder.aspx).

The Big Five Personality Traits
Personality assessments like the Big Five offer insights into how

openness to experience (one of the five traits) correlates with curiosity (https://mypersonality.net/quiz?afid=msmps&ms-clkid=1bc1bace66c21f0b8d36ddf04e8fed44).

ONLINE COURSES AND LEARNING PLATFORMS

Coursera: Courses in Design Thinking, Innovation, and Creativity
Platforms like Coursera offer specific courses on curiosity-related skills, including design thinking, which can help you approach challenges with a fresh perspective.

LinkedIn Learning: Creativity and Innovation Programs
LinkedIn Learning provides courses from industry experts on topics such as fostering curiosity, leading with innovation, and developing a growth mindset.

MasterClass: Sessions with Industry Experts on Creativity and Leadership
Featuring classes from leaders in various fields, MasterClass offers sessions that touch on creativity, curiosity, and innovation, with practical takeaways for your career.

ADDITIONAL RESOURCES AND ARTICLES

Harvard Business Review's "Curiosity and Work" Collection
https://hbr.org/2018/09/the-business-case-for-curiosity
A series of articles on the role of curiosity in the workplace, with practical strategies for leaders looking to cultivate a curious workforce.

IDEO's Design Kit
https://www.designkit.org/
A resource by IDEO, one of the leading design firms, offering a toolkit for innovation and human-centered design, perfect for teams looking to inspire creativity and curiosity.

Fast Company's Innovation Section
https://www.fastcompany.com/section/innovation
Regularly updated articles on trends in curiosity, creativity, and business innovation.

These resources offer valuable insights and practical tools to help you and your organization embrace new ideas and drive innovation.

CONNECT WITH ME

For more resources, articles, and interactive tools, visit debraclary.com. I also invite you to connect with me on social media at https://www.linkedin.com/in/drdebraclary for discussions, updates, and further tips on fostering curiosity in your work and life. Let's continue this journey together!

ACKNOWLEDGMENTS

This book would not have been possible without the unwavering support, inspiration, and encouragement of so many extraordinary individuals.

To my parents, Curt and Jean Clary, thank you for your steadfast love and the foundation of curiosity and resilience you instilled in me. To my brothers, Mark and Curt Clary, thank you for challenging me to push beyond what I thought possible as a "girl" and for always believing in my potential. Your support and constant reminders to stay curious have made all the difference.

To my daughters, Megan Clary Brownell and Madeline Clary Hueke—your brilliance, boldness, and curiosity are a daily source of inspiration. Watching you grow into the remarkable women you are today has been my greatest joy. This book, in many ways, is a love letter to the questions we've asked, the stories we've shared, and the future you continue to shape.

To the incredible team at Fast Company, I am deeply grateful for your vision, collaboration, and dedication to bringing this book to life. Your commitment to excellence elevated every page and ensured that the ideas within this book were presented with clarity and impact.

A heartfelt thank-you to Art Linker, whose invaluable guidance helped shape the concepts in this book, and to Cory and Sehyun Kim, founders of Lab 201, for their meticulous research and dedication to uncovering the insights that drive curiosity. Your work laid the groundwork for meaningful exploration.

To the healthcare organizations and leaders who participated in the Curiosity Curve assessment—thank you for your openness, your willingness to dig deep, and your commitment to exploring how curiosity can transform leadership and organizational culture. Your contributions have enriched this book in profound ways.

To my editor and the publishing team, thank you for your expertise and care and for helping me refine my voice while staying true to my vision. Your partnership has been invaluable.

Finally, to every reader, leader, and curious soul who picks up this book: Thank you for being part of this journey. Your willingness to ask questions, explore possibilities, and embrace curiosity inspires me every day.

This book is for you. May it ignite curiosity in your life and work, and may that curiosity open doors to opportunities you've never imagined.

With gratitude,
Dr. Debra Clary

NOTES

INTRODUCTION

1. "State of the Global Workplace," *Gallup*, 2024, https://www.gallup.com/workplace/349484/state-of-the-global-workplace.aspx/.
2. "Four Generations, One Workforce," *Marsh McLennan Agency*, April 18, 2024, https://www.marshmma.com/us/insights/details/generations-in-the-workplace.html/.
3. Sophie von Stumm, Benedikt Hell, and Tomas Chamorro-Premuzic, "The Hungry Mind: Intellectual Curiosity Is the Third Pillar of Academic Performance," Perspectives on Psychological Science 6, no. 6 (2011): 574–88, DOI: 10.1177/1745691611421204.
4. Sophie von Stumm, "Curiosity Is a Pillar of Academic Performance," The Psychologist 29, no. 5 (2016): 372–73.

CHAPTER 1

1. Arthur Conan Doyle, "The Adventure of Silver Blaze." In *The Memoirs of Sherlock Holmes* (G. Newnes Ltd., 1893).
2. Helen Dukas and Banesh Hoffmann, eds., *Albert Einstein: The Human Side* (Princeton University Press, 1981), 57.
3. Ivar Fahsing, "The Making of an Expert Detective: Thinking and Deciding in Criminal Investigations," Politihøgskolen, 2016, https://phs.brage.unit.no/phs-xmlui/handle/11250/2428006/.

4. Kori Miller, "5+ Ways to Develop a Growth Mindset Using Grit & Resilience," *PositivePsychology.com*, January 30, 2020, https://positivepsychology.com/5-ways-develop-grit-resilience/.
5. Ted Lasso, season 1, episode 8, "The Diamond Dogs," written by Jason Sudeikis et al., directed by Declan Lowney, aired September 18, 2020, on Apple TV+.
6. Art Kleiner, "Are We Ready for the New Culture of Empathy?," *Medium*, March 19, 2020, https://art-kleiner.medium.com/are-we-ready-for-the-new-culture-of-empathy-83f92ebeb35b/.
7. Seinfeld, season 9, episode 13, "The Cartoon," written by Larry David et al., directed by Andy Ackerman, aired January 29, 1998.
8. Saturday Night Live, season 43, episode 18, "Diner Lobster," aired April 14, 2018.
9. Ivar Fahsing, "The Making of an Expert Detective: Thinking and Deciding in Criminal Investigations," Politihøgskolen, 2016, https://phs.brage.unit.no/phs-xmlui/handle/11250/2428006/.
10. Alison Gopnik, PhD, Andrew N. Meltzoff, PhD, Patricia K. Kuhl, PhD, The Scientist in the Crib: What Early Learning Tells Us About the Mind (New York: HarperCollins, 2000).
11. Adele Gottfried et al., "Pathways from Parental Stimulation of Children's Curiosity to High School Science Course Accomplishments and Science Career Interest and Skill," *International Journal of Science Education* 38, no. 12 (2016), DOI: 10.1080/09500693.2016.1220690.
12. Joseph Luft, "The Johari Window: A Graphic Model of Awareness in Interpersonal Relations." *Human Relations Training News* 5, no. 1 (1961): 6–7, https://ombuds.columbia.edu/sites/default/files/content/pics/30%20Anniv/The%20Johari%20window_A%20graphic%20model%20of%20awareness%20in%20interpersonal%20relations.pdf.

CHAPTER 2

1. Matthias Gruber, Bernard Gelman, and Charan Ranganath, "States of Curiosity Modulate Hippocampus-Dependent Learning Via the Dopaminergic Circuit," *Neuron* 84, no. 2 (2014): 486–96, DOI: 10.1016/j.neuron.2014.08.060.

2. Anne Trafton, "Study Links Gene to Cognitive Resilience in the Elderly," *MIT News*, November 3, 2021, https://news.mit.edu/2021/gene-cognitive-resilience-elderly-1103/.
3. J. A. Litman and C. D. Spielberger, "Measuring Epistemic Curiosity and Its Diversive and Specific Components," *Journal of Personality Assessment* 80 (2003): 75–86; J. A. Litman, "Epistemic Curiosity," *Encyclopedia of the Sciences of Learning* (2012): 1162–65.
4. J. A. Litman and T. L. Jimerson, "The Measurement of Curiosity as a Feeling of Deprivation," *Journal of Personality Assessment* 82 (2004): 147–57.
5. T. B. Kashdan, P. Rose, and F. D. Fincham, "Curiosity and Exploration: Facilitating Positive Subjective Experiences and Personal Growth Opportunities," *Journal of Personality Assessment* 82 (2004): 291–305.
6. "The Curiosity Curve," *Lab 201*, August 2023; Cory Nakabayashi, "Understanding the Substrate of Organizational Curiosity: Development of the Cultural Curiosity Scale," *Lab 201*, December 10, 2022.

CHAPTER 3

1. "Survival Tips from the Pioneers," *ComputerWorld*, March 15, 2001; Paul Leinwand and Cesare Mainardi, "Frito-Lay's Identity Profile," in *Strategy That Works* (Boston: Harvard Business Review Press), 74.
2. P. Çelik, M. Storme, A. Davila, and N. Myszkowski, "Work-Related Curiosity Positively Predicts Worker Innovation," *Journal of Management Development* 35 (2016): 1184–94.
3. Todd B. Kashdan et al., "Curiosity Has Comprehensive Benefits in the Workplace: Developing and Validating a Multidimensional Workplace Curiosity Scale in United States and German Employees," *Personality and Individual Differences* 155 (2010), doi:10.1016/j.paid.2019.109717.
4. Ulrich A. K. Betz, editor, *Curious2018: Future Insights in Science and Technology* (New York: Springer, 2019).

5. Unika Prihatsanti, "The Relationship Between Entrepreneurial Self-Efficacy, Entrepreneurial Curiosity and Innovative Behavior on Entrepreneur Students," *Proceedings of the 3rd ASEAN Conference on Psychology, Counseling, and Humanities*, Atlantis Press, February 2018.
6. Art Kleiner, interview with the author, July 2024.
7. Barry Jaruzelski, Volker Staack, and Brad Goehle, "The Global Innovation 1000: Proven Paths to Innovation Success," *strategy+business* 77, 2014.

CHAPTER 4

1. Alvin Toffler, *Future Shock* (Random House, 1970), 414.
2. Argyris' theories, particularly in Chris Argyris and Donald Schön, *Theory in Practice: Increasing Professional Effectiveness* (Jossey-Bass, 1992).
3. Marie Kondo, *The Life-Changing Magic of Tidying Up: The Japanese Art of Decluttering and Organizing* (Ten Speed Press, 2014).
4. Marshall Goldsmith and Mark Reiter, *What Got You Here Won't Get You There: How Successful People Become Even More Successful* (Grand Central Publishing, 2007).
5. Alecia J. Carter et al., "Women's Visibility in Academic Seminars: Women Ask Fewer Questions than Men," *PLOS ONE* 14, no. 2 (2018), DOI: 10.1371/journal.pone.0202743.
6. Alecia J. Carter et al., "Women's Visibility in Academic Seminars: Women Ask Fewer Questions than Men," *PLOS ONE* 14, no. 2 (2018), DOI: 10.1371/journal.pone.0202743.
7. Julie Castro Abrams, interview with the author, 2024.
8. "US Corporate Board Diversity: Boards Are More Diverse than Ever, But the Pace of Growth Is Slowing," *The Conference Board*, November 9, 2023, https://www.conference-board.org/press/press-release-board-diversity-2023/.
9. Martha Burk, "Gender Diversity on California Corporate Boards Was Too Good to Last," *Ms. Magazine*, June 1, 2022, https://msmagazine.com/2022/06/01/gender-diversity-california-corporate-boards-gender-quota/.

10. Brian Melley, "Judge Says California Law Requiring Women on Corporate Boards Is Unconstitutional," *PBS News*, May 16, 2022, https://www.pbs.org/newshour/politics/judge-says-california-law-requiring-women-on-corporate-boards-is-unconstitutional/.

11. Dan Konigsburg and Sharon Thorne, "Women in the Boardroom: 2022 Update," *Harvard Law School Forum on Corporate Governance*, March 5, 2022, https://corpgov.law.harvard.edu/2022/03/05/women-in-the-boardroom-2022-update/.

12. "New Data from Deloitte and the Alliance for Board Diversity (ABD) Reveals Continued Focus Is Necessary for Fortune 500 Boards to be More Representative of the US Population," *Deloitte*, June 15, 2023, https://www2.deloitte.com/us/en/pages/about-deloitte/articles/press-releases/new-data-reveals-opportunity-for-growth-on-fortune-500-boards-to-be-more-representative-of-the-us-population.html/.

13. How Women Invest, https://www.howwomeninvest.com/.

CHAPTER 5

1. Tracy Rector, interview with the author, June 2024.

2. Harry McCracken, "How Gmail Happened: The Inside Story of Its Launch 10 Years Ago," *Time magazine*, April 1, 2014, https://time.com/43263/gmail-10th-anniversary/.

3. Lab 201, "Cultural Curiosity Scale Follow-up: A Practical Review of the Cultural Curiosity Scale," prepared by Cory Kim, June 2025.

CHAPTER 6

1. Nina Esaki, Xiaofang Liu, and Rosemary Vito, "An Exploratory Study of Employee Engagement in Human Service Agencies," *Journal of Human Services* 43, no. 1 (2023), https://journalhumanservices.org/article/89008-an-exploratory-study-of-employee-engagement-in-human-service-agencies/.

2. "The Benefits of Employee Engagement," *Gallup*, January 7, 2023, https://www.gallup.com/workplace/236927/employee-engagement-drives-growth.aspx/.

3. William Kahn, "Psychological conditions of personal engagement and disengagement at work," *Academy of Management Journal*, 33, (1990): 692–724
4. Ron Ricci, interview with the author, June 2024.
5. Mike Cunnion, interview with the author, June 2024.
6. Naresh Sekar, "Patagonia (Don't Buy This Jacket)," *Medium.com*, June 27, 2024, https://medium.com/%40nareshnavinash/patagonia-dont-buy-this-jacket-027c554345c5/.

CHAPTER 7

1. Lab 201, "Cultural Curiosity Scale Follow-up: A Practical Review of the Cultural Curiosity Scale," prepared by Cory Kim, June 2025.

CHAPTER 8

1. Dr. Joan Kelly, interview with the author, June 2024.
2. "Yale School of Medicine Adapts to the COVID-19 Pandemic," *Yale School of Medicine*, January/February 2021, https://medicine.yale.edu/news/medicineatyale/article/yale-school-of-medicine-adapts-to-the-covid19/.
3. Lab 201, "Cultural Curiosity Scale Follow-up: A Practical Review of the Cultural Curiosity Scale," prepared by Cory Kim, June 2025.

INDEX

A

absorption, 49–50
accessibility, leadership, 134–35
active listening, 101–2
adaptability of organizations, 126, 136, 162, 166–67, 176
"The Adventure of Silver Blaze" (Holmes), 19
after-action reviews, 166
Apple, 14, 22, 79
Argyris, Chris, 105
The Art of Asking (Ted Talk), 184–85
assessing curiosity in leaders, 92–94

B

Berkshire Hathaway, 14
Big Five Personality Traits, 185–86
Blockbuster, 14
books about curiosity, 183–84
brain, function of curiosity in, 44–47
Buffett, Warren, 14
business, impact of curiosity on
  adaptability, 126, 136, 162, 166–67, 176
  benefits of curious culture, 67
  commitment, 69–72
  curiosity setpoint, 76–78
  employee retention, 72–78
  at Frito-Lay, 61–66
  innovation, 67–69
  key insights, 83
  optimal level of curiosity, finding, 78–80
  reflection questions, 80–82
  resilience, 69, 126, 143
business strategies, 180–81

C

California Senate Bill 826 (SB 826), 112
Capra, Frank, 29
Castro Abrams, Julie, 110–16
cat not killed by curiosity, 35–37
CCS. *See* Cultural Curiosity Scale
CEI (curiosity and exploration inventory), 49–50, 52–53, 77
CFD (curiosity as a feeling of deprivation) scale, 49, 77–78
childhood, curiosity in, 30–31, 38
Chouinard, Yvon, 14
Christensen, Clayton, 183
Cisco, 144
Clary, Debra, 184

clear intentions, setting, 145
Coca-Cola, 71–72
cognitive resilience, 46
collaboration
   cross-departmental, 125, 130
   cross-functional, 125–26, 133, 134, 138
   experimentation, rewarding, 132
   focused engagement for teams, 141–42, 147–53
   fostering culture of curiosity, 9–15, 69
   inspiring creativity in teams, 164–65
   team exploration, encouraging, 125–26, 130–32
   time management tools, 152
collaboration sessions, 130
commitment, impact of curiosity on, 69–72
communication protocols, establishing, 153, 155–56
conferences, attending, 127–28, 163–64
confirmation bias, 33
contagiousness of curiosity, 37, 44, 76
continuous learning, 126, 127
core values, embedding curiosity in, 126, 135
Coursera, 186
COVID-19 pandemic, 172–73
Creative Solution Awards, 165
creativity, inspirational
   assessing curiosity in leaders, 93
   creative skill development, encouraging, 163
   curiosity linked to, 20–21
   general discussion, 87–90
   impact on growth, 90–91
   in individuals, 162–64
   in organizations, 166–68
   overview, 18, 85, 161–62
   reflection questions, 168–69
   in teams, 164–65
creativity zones, 166
cross-cultural experiences, supporting, 175
cross-departmental collaboration, 125, 130
cross-functional collaboration, 125–26, 133, 134, 138
Cultural Curiosity Scale (CCS)
   creation of, 54–56
   employee engagement and, 70–71
   items on, 55

job satisfaction and, 12
job tenure and, 73–74
culture of curiosity
   assessing curiosity in leaders, 92–94
   benefits of, 67
   commitment and, 69–72
   curiosity setpoint, 76–78
   employee retention and, 72–78
   fostering, 9–15, 38–39
   at Frito-Lay, 61–66
   innovation and, 67–69
   key insights, 83
   modeling curiosity, 38–39
   optimal level of curiosity, finding, 78–80
   reflection questions, 80–82
Cunnion, Mike, 148–49
Curie, Marie, 21–22, 23
curiosity. *See also* culture of curiosity; signs of curiosity
   brain function and, 44–47
   cat not killed by, 35–37
   curiosity gap, 30–35
   in democracies, 14
   discoveries and growth through, 6–9
   Johari Window model, 33–35
   key insights, 41
   killers of, 36–37
   measures of, 47–51
   optimal, 51–54
   overview, 19–20
   reflection questions, 40
   role in success, 13
   stifling of, 10–11
   takeaway, 37–38
   as trait vs. skill, 20–24
   transformative power of, 1–6
   as way of life, 38–41
curiosity and exploration inventory (CEI), 49–50, 52–53, 77
"Curiosity and Work" Collection, *Harvard Business Review*'s, 186
curiosity as a feeling of deprivation (CFD) scale, 49, 77–78
curiosity budget, 128, 139
"curiosity corners," setting up, 163
Curiosity Curve. *See also* curiosity growth factors
   impact on growth, 90–91
   overview, 12–13
   Self-Assessment, 185
curiosity gap, 30–35, 39
curiosity growth factors. *See also*

exploration; focused engagement; inspirational creativity; openness to new ideas
  assessing curiosity in leaders, 92–94
  and employee engagement, 90–91
  general discussion, 87–90
  impact on growth, 90–91
  reflection questions, 116–19
  women as curious leaders, 108–16
"curiosity killed the cat," 35–37
curiosity library, 131–32
curiosity setpoint, 76–78
Curiosity: Two Truths & A Lie (Ted Talk), 184
curiosity workshops, 131
curious leaders
  active listening, practicing, 101–2
  assessing, 92–94
  feedback, embracing, 102–3
  hypotheses, forming and testing, 104
  learning to project curiosity, 94–97
  open-ended questions, asking, 97–101
  unlearning, 105–8
  women as, 108–16
A Curious Mind: The Secret to a Bigger Life (Grazer & Fishman), 184

D

Davidson, Pete, 29
decluttering, 105–6
dementia prevention, 46
democracy, role of curiosity in, 14
deprivation, curiosity as feeling of, 49
Design Kit, IDEO's, 187
design thinking techniques, using, 164
"digital detox" practices, encouraging, 155
disengagement, costs of employee, 11
disruption caused by curiosity, 26–28
distractions, eliminating, 145
diverse learning experiences, encouraging, 163–64
diversity initiatives, promoting, 166
"dogs that don't bark," 17, 19–20
domestic violence, film about, 121–22
"Don't Buy This Jacket" campaign, Patagonia, 149–50
dress code at schools, 32–33

Duckworth, Angela, 184
Dweck, Carol, 22–23

E

EC (epistemic curiosity) scale, 47–48
Einstein, Albert, 21–22, 23
email protocols, establishing, 153, 155
empathy, as sign of curiosity, 25–26
employee engagement. *See also* focused engagement
  costs of disengagement, 11
  Cultural Curiosity Scale and, 12, 70–71
  curiosity culture and, 69–72
  curiosity growth factors and, 90–91
  disengagement, costs of, 11
employees. *See also* teams
  commitment of, 69–72
  curiosity setpoint, 76–78
  focused engagement of individual, 141–47
  individual exploration, encouraging, 125, 127–29
  innovation and curiosity of, 67–69
  inspiring creativity in individual, 162–64
  matching curiosity of culture, 94–95
  openness to new ideas in, 174–76
  retention of, 72–78
entrepreneurship in women, 110–16
epistemic curiosity (EC) scale, 47–48
Epstein, David, 184
ergonomic workspaces, investing in, 156
experience sharing, 25–26
experimentation, culture of, 133, 138
exploration
  assessing curiosity in leaders, 92
  benefits of, 126–27
  curiosity and exploration inventory, 49–50, 52–53, 77
  fostering, 125–26
  general discussion, 87–90
  harnessing curiosity for, 124–39
  hiring process at Google, 123–24
  impact on growth, 90–91
  individual, encouraging, 127–29
  organizational, encouraging, 132–36
  overview, 18, 85

Index 199

reflection questions, 137–39
team, encouraging, 129–32
Tracy Rector's creative leap, 121–23
exploration fund, creating, 134
eye contact, 102

F

Fahsing, Ivar, 21–22, 29
failures, learning from, 166
Fast Company, 187
feedback, embracing, 102–3, 135
Fincham, Frank, 49–50
Fishman, Charles, 184
flexible promotional pricing, 65–66
flow state, 146
fMRI (functional magnetic resonance imaging) scans, 45–46
focused achievements, recognizing and rewarding, 156–59
focused engagement
　assessing curiosity in leaders, 93
　examples of, 146–47
　general discussion, 87–90
　impact on growth, 90–91
　at individual level, 142–47
　at organization level, 153–59
　overview, 18, 85, 141–59
　reflection questions, 158–59
　at team level, 147–53
focus hours, 150–51, 154
focus times, personalized, 154
Ford, Henry, 174
Fortune 500 Board Data, 112–13
Frito-Lay, 1–4, 61–66
functional magnetic resonance imaging (fMRI) scans, 45–46
future of curiosity, 179–82
Future Shock (Toffler), 105

G

gender differences in curiosity, 108–9
genuine questions, 98–101
goals for teams, 151
Goldsmith, Marshall, 106
Google, 123–24
Gopnik, Alison, 30–31

Grant, Adam, 184
Grazer, Brian, 184, 185
Great Resignation of 2022–2023, 11
Grit: The Power of Passion and Perseverance (Ted Talk), 184
group learning sessions, 131
groupthink, 33
growth
　curiosity growth factors, 87–90
　impact of curiosity on, 90–91
growth mindset, 22–23

H

hackathons, organizing, 165
Harvard Business Review's "Curiosity and Work" Collection, 186
Harvard Law School's "Women in the Boardroom" report, 112
healthcare technology company, 10
hesitation among women, 108–10
hippocampus, 46
hiring process at Google, 123–24
Holmes, Sherlock, 19
How Women Invest, 110–16
How Women Lead, 110–16
Humana, 43–44
humor, as sign of curiosity, 29
hypotheses, forming and testing, 104

I

ice ball incident, 26–28
idea exchanges, 125–26
idea jams, 131
"ideas portal," launching, 167
IDEO's Design Kit, 187
IKEA, 174
inclusion initiatives, promoting, 166
individual level
　exploration, encouraging, 125, 127–29
　focused engagement at, 141–47
　inspiring creativity at, 162–64
　openness to new ideas at, 174–76
industry news and research, open access to, 129
Ingham, Harrington, 33–35

innovation. *See also* inspirational creativity
 celebrating individual achievements in, 163
 challenges, organizing, 165
 conducting regular workshops in, 164
 fostering culture of curiosity, 9–15
 "Innovation Awards" ceremony, 167
 innovation days, 126, 134, 139
 innovation hours, 162
 innovation lab, 133
 Innovator of the Month, 163
 recognition programs for, 167–69
 role of curiosity in, 67–69
Innovation 1000, 79
The Innovator's Dilemma (Christensen), 183
inspirational creativity
 assessing curiosity in leaders, 93
 general discussion, 87–90
 impact on growth, 90–91
 in individuals, 162–64
 in organizations, 166–68
 overview, 18, 85, 161–62
 reflection questions, 168–69
 in teams, 164–65
inspiring curiosity, 37
internal curiosity, 29–30
intrinsic motivation, 68
investing in women entrepreneurs, 113–14
irritation caused by curiosity, 26

J

Jaruzelski, Barry, 79
Jimerson, Tiffany, 49
job satisfaction
 CEI charted against, 52–53
 Cultural Curiosity Scale and, 12
 employee engagement and, 142–43
job shadowing opportunities, 128, 131
Jobs, Steve, 14, 21–22, 23
job tenure
 commitment and, 69–72
 cultural curiosity and, 72–76
 curiosity setpoint and, 77–78
Johari Window model, 33–35
jokes, as sign of curiosity, 29
Journal of Human Services, 142–43

K

Kashdan, Todd, 49–50
Kelly, Joan, 172–73
killers of curiosity, 36–37
Kim, Cory, 12, 54. *See also* Cultural Curiosity Scale
Kleiner, Art, 68–69
knowledge-sharing, 69, 128–29, 133
Kodak, 14
Kondo, Marie, 105–6
Kuhl, Patricia, 30–32

L

Lab 201, 11–12, 43, 54, 67, 69, 83, 94
 See also Cultural Curiosity Scale
Lasso, Ted, 24
leadership. *See also* exploration; focused engagement; inspirational creativity; openness to new ideas
 active listening, practicing, 101–2
 assessing curiosity in leaders, 92–94
 feedback, embracing, 102–3
 hypotheses, forming and testing, 104
 impact of fostering curiosity, 180
 learning to project curiosity, 94–97
 modeling curiosity, 38–39
 open-ended questions, asking, 97–101
 optimal levels of curiosity, 51–54
 power of questions, 63–64
 transparency and accessibility, promoting, 134–35
 unlearning, 105–8
 women as curious leaders, 108–16
learning
 continuous, 126, 127
 diverse experiences, encouraging, 163–64
 from failures, 166
 learning days, 127
 learning sessions, 131
 lifelong, encouraging, 175
 lunch and learns, 131
 to project curiosity, 94–97
 resources for, 186
 self-directed, 127
 "lessons learned" session, 166
lifelong learning, encouraging, 175

LinkedIn Learning, 186
listening, active, 101–2
Litman, Jordan, 47–48, 49
Luft, Joseph, 33–35
lunch and learns, 131

M

MasterClass, 186
measures of curiosity, 47–51
meditation for unlearning, 106–8
Meltzoff, Andrew, 30–31
mentalizing, 25–26
mentorship, 128, 166
mesencephalon, 45–46
metacognition, 22, 29
midbrain, 45–46
millennials, disengagement among, 11
mindfulness
    breaks for teams, 152–53
    and focus training, integrating, 154
    practicing, 145
modeling curiosity, 37, 38–39
Mulaney, John, 29

N

nature of curiosity. See also signs of curiosity
    cat not killed by, 35–37
    curiosity as way of life, 38–41
    curiosity gap, 30–35
    key insights, 41
    killers of, 36–37
    overview, 19–20
    reflection questions, 40
    takeaway, 37–38
    as trait vs. skill, 20–24
Need Seekers, 79
networking events, attending, 175
neuroscience of curiosity
    brain function and, 44–47
    Cultural Curiosity Scale, 54–56
    measures of curiosity, 47–51
    optimal curiosity, 51–54
    overview, 43–44
    reflection questions, 57–59
new product launches, 1–4

"no-meeting" days, implementing, 154
nongenuine questions, 98–101
No Ordinary Love (film), 121–23
nucleus accumbens, 46

O

office spaces, designing, 156, 166
online courses, 186
open-ended questions, asking, 97–101
open idea submissions, 135
openness to new ideas
    assessing curiosity in leaders, 93
    fostering, 174
    general discussion, 87–90
    impact on growth, 90–91
    at individual level, 175-76
    learning to project curiosity, 94–97
    overview, 18, 85, 171–72
    reflection questions, 177-78
optimal level of curiosity
    finding, 78–80
    general discussion, 51–54
organization level
    exploration, encouraging, 126, 132–36
    focused engagement at, 142, 153–57
    inspiring creativity in, 166–68
Originals: How Non-Conformists Move the World (Grant), 184

P

Palmer, Amanda, 184–85
parents, fostering curiosity in children, 31–32, 38
passion projects, 129, 162
Patagonia, 14, 149–50
personal growth, 144
personalized focus times, offering flexibility for, 154
personal projects, allocating time for, 162
popping and lacing, 62
The Power of Curiosity (podcast), 185
power of questions, 62–64
prioritization workshops, 150

problems, resolving with curiosity, 104, 143, 165
Procter & Gamble, 79
project management tools, leveraging for clarity, 155
promotional pricing, 65–66
Prototype Day, 165
prototyping, culture of, 133, 138, 165
psychological safety, 130, 137
pub trivia nights study, 45–46
PwC, 68–69

Q

questions
   for feedback, 103
   fostering culture of curiosity, 9–15
   genuine versus nongenuine, 98–101
   open-ended, asking, 97–101
   power of, 62–64
   as sign of curiosity, 25
"quiet quitting" movement, 11
quiet zones, designating, 153–54

R

Range: Why Generalists Triumph in a Specialized World (Epstein), 184
reading outside of field, 176–77
recognition
   celebrating individual achievements in innovation, 163
   of focused achievements, 156–59
   for innovation, 167–69
   of knowledge-sharing, 133
Rector, Tracy, 121–24
reflection, as sign of curiosity, 29–30
reflection practices, incorporating regular, 175
reflective meditation for unlearning, 106–8
Remedy Health Media, 148–49
research and development (R&D) spending, 79
resilience, 69, 125, 143
resistance to curiosity, 13
resources, 183–87
response times, setting for teams, 153
retention of employees
   commitment and curiosity, 69–72

cultural curiosity and, 72–76
curiosity setpoint and, 77–78
reverse mentoring, 126, 128
rewarding
   creative problem-solving, 165
   experimentation, 132
   focused achievements, 156–59
   knowledge-sharing, 133
Ricci, Ron, 144
Robinson, Chyna, 122–23
Rose, Paul, 49–50
rotation programs, 130
route drivers at Frito-Lay, 1–4, 61–66

S

SafeHaven, 121–22
schools, curiosity stifled at, 32–33
Schultz, Howard, 173
self-assessments and tools, 185–86
self-directed learning, 127
Senate Bill 826 (SB 826), California, 112
Shakespeare, William, 35
side projects, 125
signs of curiosity
   disruption people cause, 26–28
   empathy people feel, 25–26
   irritation people tolerate, 26
   jokes people tell, 29
   overview, 24
   questions people ask, 25
   way people reflect, 29–30
   words people use, 24–25
single-tasking culture, 151
skill, curiosity as, 20–24, 43–44
small wins, celebrating, 146
Spielberger, Charles, 47–48
sprint intervals, 152
Starbucks, 173
start, stop, and continue team exercises, 151
storytelling sessions, 165
strategic stretch goals, setting, 133
strategy+business (magazine), 68–69
Strengths Finder by Gallup, 185
stretch assignments, 127
stretch goals, setting, 133
subscriptions to industry publications, 129
success, role of curiosity in, 13

T

task batching, promoting, 155
teams
   cross-departmental collaboration, 125, 130
   cross-functional collaboration, 125–26, 133, 134, 138
   exploration, encouraging, 125–26, 129–32
   focused engagement for, 141–42, 147–53
   inspiring creativity in, 164–65
   reaching out to in curiosity, 4–5
   task batching, promoting, 155
"tech-free" rooms, 155
Tesla, 79
time-blocking, 145
time management tools, 152
Toffler, Alvin, 105
training and development programs, 135–36
trait, curiosity as skill vs., 20–24
transparency, leadership, 134–35
travel, supporting, 175
trust, 13

U

unlearning, 105–8

V

values, embedding curiosity in organizational, 126, 135
varsity basketball tryout, 6–9

venture fund capital investing, 113–14
virtual talks, 184–85

W

way of life, curiosity as, 38–41
women
   business impact of curiosity in, 115–16
   on corporate boards, 110–13
   hesitation to speak up in, 108–10
   "How Women Lead" discussion series, 114–15
   investing in, 113–14
   "Women in the Boardroom" report, Harvard Law School, 112
   Women's Initiative for Self Employment, 110–11
words people use, as sign of curiosity, 24–25
workshop attendance, sponsoring, 127
workspaces, designing, 156, 166

Y

Yale New Haven Health System, 172–73

Z

Zaki, Jamil, 25

ABOUT THE AUTHOR

Dr. Debra Clary is a narrative scientist and transformational leader with a remarkable journey—from the Frito-Lay route truck to the corporate boardroom. With more than three decades of executive experience at Fortune 50 companies, she now serves as founder and CEO of The Clary Group, where her team ignites curiosity-driven mindsets to accelerate personal growth, enhance team performance, and spark organizational innovation.

She has held leadership roles at some of the world's most recognized brands, including Frito-Lay, Coca-Cola, Jack Daniel's, and Humana. Across each, Debra mastered the ability to navigate complex systems through a lens of curiosity and strategic thinking. Her rare blend of innovation and grounded leadership insights has made her a trusted advisor, speaker, and thought leader across industries.

A viral TEDx speaker, international keynote presenter, author, and award-winning film producer, Debra captivates audiences with her storytelling and stage presence. In 2023, she brought her signature storytelling to life in the Off-Broadway solo performance *A Curious Woman*—a theatrical expression of her belief in the power of narrative to connect and transform.

Debra earned her doctorate in leader development, change management, and organizational design from The George Washington University, where she received the prestigious Ralph Stone Leadership Award for excellence in leadership studies. Her life's work is a testament to the transformative power of curiosity—fueling growth, innovation, and human connection across every level of an organization.

Praise for *The Curiosity Curve*

"In a world where change is constant and certainty is fleeting, curiosity has become a non-negotiable leadership skill. In *The Curiosity Curve*, Debra Clary masterfully shows how cultivating curiosity can transform how we lead, connect, and grow. Her insights are timely, practical, and deeply human—this book is an indispensable resource for anyone who wants to coach with intention in today's complex world."

—MARSHALL GOLDSMITH, *New York Times* #1 best-selling author of *The Earned Life* and *What Got You Here Won't Get You There*

"Years ago, I asked Deb Clary a simple question: 'Is curiosity learned or innate?' She turned that moment into a movement. In *The Curiosity Curve*, she explores curiosity as a critical leadership competency—one that fuels innovation, empathy, and resilience. A timely reminder that the leaders of tomorrow won't be those with the best answers—but those with the boldest questions."

—BRUCE BROUSSARD, former CEO, Humana Inc.

"In today's technology-driven economy, innovation isn't just about products—it's about people. *The Curiosity Curve* brilliantly captures how curiosity fuels the skills, mindset, and culture needed to stay competitive."

—CHRIS ROARK, senior managing director, Accenture

"Curiosity isn't just a soft skill—it's the driving force behind the most innovative leaders, entrepreneurs, and change-makers. In *The Curiosity Curve*, Debra Clary masterfully unpacks how curiosity fuels breakthrough thinking, deepens connections, and drives game-changing results. This book is a must-read for anyone looking to challenge the status quo and unlock their full creative potential."

—**JOSH LINKNER**, *New York Times* best-selling author, tech entrepreneur, and innovation expert

"In *The Curiosity Curve*, Debra Clary reveals what many leaders miss—curiosity is not a nice-to-have, it's a must-have. With real-world insight and inspiring clarity, she shows how the most effective leaders lead with questions, not just answers. This book is a powerful guide for anyone who wants to build stronger teams, a culture of accountability, and a bolder business."

—**JULIA STEWART**, founder and CEO, Alurx; former chair and CEO, Dine Brands Global

"In *The Curiosity Curve*, Debra Clary makes a compelling case that curiosity is the foundation of positive leadership. She brilliantly illustrates how the most effective leaders don't just seek answers—they cultivate a mindset of exploration that fuels growth, innovation, and deep human connection. This book is both a call to action and a practical guide for anyone looking to lead with greater purpose, adaptability, and impact."

—**DR. ROBERT E. QUINN**, professor emeritus, University of Michigan; cofounder, Center for Positive Organizations

"Most of us are unaware of the amazing power and transforming benefits of curiosity. In this fabulous book, Dr. Clary shows how you can develop this wonderful trait/tool to change your life and the lives of the people around you. *The Curiosity Curve* is a must-read for anyone seeking to be a better leader, a better friend, and a better person."

—**DR. MICHAEL MARQUARDT**, professor emeritus, George Washington University; author of the global bestseller *Leading with Questions*

"Great leaders aren't just great talkers—they're great listeners, great learners, and deeply curious about the world around them. In *The Curiosity Curve*, Debra Clary brilliantly unpacks how curiosity fuels breakthrough thinking, deepens connections, and transforms leadership. This book is a must-read for anyone looking to elevate their influence, sharpen their thinking, and lead with greater impact."

—**SCOTT WEISS**, chairman of Speakeasy, leadership coach, and author of *Dare!*

"In *The Curiosity Curve*, Dr. Debra Clary brilliantly illustrates how curiosity is the key to unlocking innovation, deepening relationships, and driving meaningful leadership impact. With compelling research and real-world insights, she challenges us to move beyond passive observation and embrace curiosity as a strategic advantage. A must-read for leaders, teams, and anyone looking to thrive in an ever-changing world."

—**MIKE DULWORTH**, CEO, Executive Networks; author of *The Connect Effect*

"In *The Curiosity Curve*, Debra Clary shows us why curiosity is clearly a skill and approach that modern leaders can't afford to ignore. With insight drawn from decades inside top organizations and backed by research, this book is both practical and inspiring. It's an essential read for leaders looking to build stronger teams, cultures, and outcomes."

—**TIM HUVAL,** former chief administrative officer, Humana